REAL-LIFE STORIES ABOUT

ANXIETY

FREAKiNG
OUT

POLLY WELLS

Illustrated by Peter Mitchell

annick press
toronto + new york + vancouver

A sincere thank you to Stacie B. Isenberg, Psy.D., for her contributions
and expertise.

We acknowledge the support of the Canada Council for the Arts, the Ontario
Arts Council, and the Government of Canada through the Canada Book Fund
(CBF) for our publishing activities.

ONTARIO ARTS COUNCIL
CONSEIL DES ARTS DE L'ONTARIO
50 YEARS OF ONTARIO GOVERNMENT SUPPORT OF THE ARTS
50 ANS DE SOUTIEN DU GOUVERNEMENT DE L'ONTARIO AUX ARTS

Cataloging in Publication

   Freaking out : real-life stories about anxiety / Polly Wells ;
illustrated by Peter Mitchell.

Includes bibliographical references.
Issued also in electronic formats.
ISBN 978-1-55451-545-5 (bound).—ISBN 978-1-55451-544-8 (pbk.)

   1. Anxiety in adolescence—Case studies—Juvenile literature.
2. Anxiety—Case studies—Juvenile literature. 3. Stress in adolescence—
Case studies—Juvenile literature. I. Wells, Mary Paul II. Mitchell, Peter, 1978-

BF724.3.A57F74 2013   j158.10835   C2013-901377-6

Distributed in Canada by:
Firefly Books Ltd.
50 Staples Avenue, Unit 1
Richmond Hill, ON
L4B 1H1

Published in the U.S.A. by:
Annick Press (U.S.) Ltd.
Distributed in the U.S.A. by:
Firefly Books (U.S.) Inc.
P.O. Box 1338, Ellicott Station
Buffalo, NY 14205

Printed in Canada

Visit us at: www.annickpress.com
Visit Peter Mitchell at: www.petermitchell.net

MIX
Paper from
responsible sources
FSC
www.fsc.org   FSC® C004071

ANCIENT FOREST ™
FRIENDLY

Contents

Introduction

WHY AM I FREAKING OUT?

That sweaty, gut-clenching, suffocating, racing-heart feeling. That I-can't-catch-my-breath, panicky feeling. That I-can't-stop-thinking-about-this feeling. That I-am-desperate-to-run-away or I'm-too-scared-to-move feeling. Or that dull, never-ending sense that there's something wrong. What is it? Anxiety.

But what is anxiety?

To answer this question, it can be helpful to compare anxiety to fear. So what's the difference between anxiety and fear? Well, if you're hiking on a narrow trail in the mountains in the rain, your heart might be pounding because you're *afraid* you'll fall. If you're at home in bed and your heart's pounding because you're thinking about how on a camping trip you might take someday, there might be a steep path, and you might fall on it, and you might break your leg, and it won't heal, that's *anxiety*.

Fear is a response to a *known or actual* danger or threat. Anxiety is a response to a *possible or imagined* danger or threat. The physical and emotional reactions caused by both fear and anxiety may be very similar, but what sets them off is different.

Anxiety (or worrying) is with us from the time we're babies and cry when our parents are out of sight. As we get a little older, our imagination can take us into strange territory—seeing the monster under the bed, the dragon in the closet. But just when we put those fears to rest, a new crop takes their place: the monster gives way to worry about not fitting in at school.

Nobody can escape feeling anxious

In fact, we're hardwired to have a certain amount of anxiety so that we stay safe. Worried about getting hit by a car? That makes you look both ways. It also helps us focus on what's important to us. Worried about failing a math test? That makes you pay attention in class and study.

Sometimes you feel anxiety for no apparent reason, and alleviating it isn't as simple as studying or looking around before stepping into the street. Life can throw some mean punches, and your anxiety level about that can reach the stratosphere. Anxiety might be a natural response to the biggies that life can hand you, like the death of a parent or endless bullying or heavy pressures in school.

Anxiety can be worse when you're in your teens

When you get to be a teenager, anxiety becomes the new normal. So many rapid changes are occurring in your body and brain, pretty much everyone feels it. You're more self-aware than you used to be, and that's good. It means you're ready to begin taking care of yourself. But there's a downside: The stakes are higher. Family life can get rockier because you and your parents have to figure out ways for you to take on more adult rights and responsibilities, like driving and sharing the chores. Schoolwork is harder, and it matters more: doing well in school can translate into a good job later.

Having friends also gets more complicated as hormones kick in and love enters the picture. The fact is, it's hard to navigate school, to please your parents, and to make and keep good friends. It's hard to recognize and stand up to peer pressure around being cool, sex, alcohol, and drugs. No wonder anxiety is a part of growing up.

Sometimes there's no obvious reason to be anxious, but you still feel it like a straightjacket, cheating you out of enjoying your life. That's when it's time to worry about being worried—and to do something about it. That could mean telling someone you trust or asking to see a counselor.

We all experience anxiety, but it's a sliding scale. Some of us have temperaments that make us less anxious; others seem preset to have a lot more. Neurology and genetics definitely play a role: it's common for anxiety to run in families, for example. But what happens to us as kids, and the environment we grow up in, can also cause the scale to tilt in a negative direction. Even a small tendency to worry can erupt into full-blown panic if our lives go a certain way and we don't get help.

The thirteen young people who tell their stories here all coped with excessive anxiety when they were teens. Each of them faced periods of extreme stress, and each of them found a way to manage that stress and move beyond it. Things *did* get better.

These stories are tough but they're also hopeful. Although it's hard to believe when anxiety has you in its grip, there *are* ways to eliminate, or at least to diminish, it. The first step to overcoming excessive anxiety is recognizing what it is.

If you suffer from anxiety, or think that you might, I hope that reading these stories will help you see that it doesn't have to take over your mind or prevent you from living your life fully. You can live with far less (or even none) of that sweaty, gut-clenching, suffocating, heart-racing feeling.

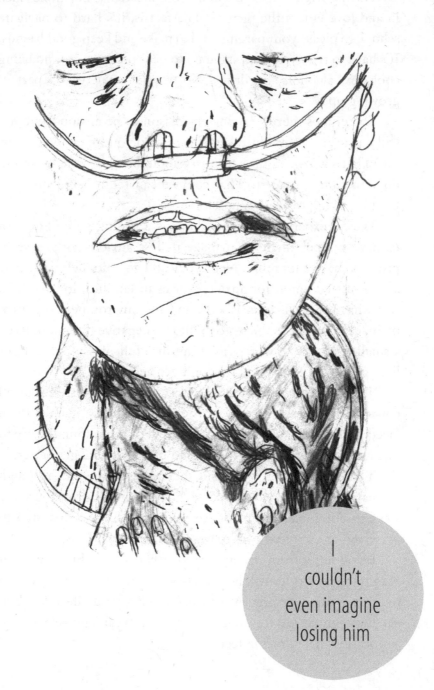

I
couldn't
even imagine
losing him

Heavy Losses

CELIA

I have so many happy memories of my childhood, tearing around the neighborhood with a pack of kids, darting in and out of one another's houses. The families on our street looked out for one another. In winter we'd play hockey on backyard rinks and go sledding in the park. In summer we'd run through sprinklers, screaming for joy, or splash around in the huge plastic pool that my dad filled up for us every June. Then when I was ten, everything changed. The years that came after were full of longing for what I had lost.

The first loss was huge, as huge as my dad. He was a mountain of a man, three hundred pounds and six-and-a-half feet tall. He was also the gentlest person ever. When I was afraid of huge dogs or scary dreams, he was there to protect me. The safest place in the world was sitting on our saggy leather couch, his giant arms wrapped around my big sister, my little brother, and me. He made up hilarious stories and pretend-wrestled us until we gasped from laughing. Sometimes at dinner, out of the blue, he'd look around and tell us he was the luckiest man in the world.

The unthinkable

My dad was a heavy smoker but we were completely taken aback when he developed lung cancer. When he told us, my sister cried and my brother didn't understand. I wasn't afraid because I couldn't even imagine losing him. That winter was bitter and stormy. On snow days, when I didn't have to go to school, he'd take me to chemo with him. Afterward we'd go to our favorite diner for fried chicken. It became normal for me. I knew cancer was bad but I always thought, *My dad's not going to die. He's a superhero. When I get older, I'm going to tell people that my dad survived lung cancer and it's going to be pretty awesome.*

That spring I turned eleven, and my dad had many weeks of radiation treatment. Then, in June, he had a seizure while bringing the groceries in from the car. I was terrified. Mom drove him to the hospital while we waited at home into the evening. My sister made us tomato soup and grilled-cheese sandwiches that I couldn't eat. When Mom came home, she looked totally wiped. She sat us down and explained that the cancer had spread to Dad's brain. He would be coming home from the hospital to die. We freaked out, wailing and shrieking. She said he wanted to be with us and didn't have much time left. He would need lots of peace and quiet.

School had just ended for the summer and the house was anything but quiet. Dad's oxygen machine beeped constantly and made a god-awful whirring noise. We were smack in the middle of a huge heat wave and our air conditioner was broken. Fans buzzed day and night. We kept all the lights off and the blinds closed. When our clothes got soaked with sweat, my mom did another load of laundry and the noise of the machine shook the floor. Dad couldn't climb the stairs anymore so he rested on the recliner in the living room. If I sat on the leather couch, I had to peel myself off, so I lay on the carpet next to him with my arms and legs spread out. The first week Dad joked and told stories. The second week he fell into a deep sleep and never woke up.

My mortality thing

A few weeks after the funeral, my mom went through the house like a roadrunner, packing up Dad's things. "I can't stand that his clothes are here and he's not," she told us. We each got to pick things to keep. I chose his football jersey and his favorite sweater. On bad days I wrapped them around me, comforted by the familiar smell of tobacco and soap.

A lot of kids have an immortality thing. They think they're invincible. I never felt that. From age eleven on, death was real to me. Our grief was like an invisible elephant in the room. A lot of our family conversations involved my dad. "Remember when we went there and Daddy said—?" Just mentioning his name would make us go quiet. The sadness was so heavy we'd each have to go away and deal with it. It felt so personal we didn't want to talk about it. Without meaning to, we were drifting apart.

Any kind of loss filled me with dread. My grandmother sold her farm and it felt like I'd lost another living breathing thing. My best friend was late to meet me at the mall, and by the time she showed up, I was shaking, convinced she'd been kidnapped.

It got so that every time my mom left the house, I wanted to throw my arms around her knees, like I used to when the babysitter came. Even if it was only a quick trip to the grocery store, I'd get a wave of panic in my chest. *What if she gets into a car accident? What if that was the last time I'll ever see her?*

"Dealing" with the grief

When I was thirteen my mom and I had a big blowup. You'd think that after what happened to my dad, she'd have quit smoking. She had even promised she would, ceremonially destroying her carton of cigarettes right after he died. Then I caught her in the backyard with a pack of cigarettes. I had a screaming fit. "How could you do this? Don't you realize this is what killed Daddy? Do you want us to be orphans? Don't you love us anymore?" I was convinced she wanted to die.

My mom listened but didn't say a word. I ran upstairs and grabbed a pair of scissors and tried to cut my arm. The scissors were dull and they only scratched my skin so I fished around in the sewing box until I found a sharper pair. This time I could feel the sting and I cried out. I stared at the beads of blood as they appeared. Seeing the blood made me feel calm in a weird way, like I had punished my mom for betraying me.

The cutting went on for about six months. When my best friend, Meggie, and I had sleepovers, I wore long-sleeved T-shirts to hide the scabs on my arms. But on Halloween, I was wearing a sheer Cleopatra costume and Meggie saw the marks. She reamed me out and threatened to tell my mom and my teachers.

I stopped the cutting, not because she threatened me, but because talking to her about it made me feel better. She helped me see that I wasn't punishing anyone but myself. We stayed up many nights talking about my issues. I feel guilty now for not ever listening to her problems!

Yet another crisis

The dread of more loss had become a part of me in all kinds of ways. I had a hard time giving away clothes I'd outgrown. I kept every drawing my brother made. I would read the end of a book to see if the hero survived, and if not, I put the book away.

School helped take my mind off my anxieties a little bit, though. I have a really good memory and can look at something a couple of times and get it. With minimal studying I was on the honor roll, getting straight As. That is, until high school, when I took Calculus. There's no way to coast through that. It takes diligent practice: you have to do the problems over and over again. But I was used to relying on my smarts, not hard work, and my grade started to plummet. I couldn't concentrate and began to have anxiety attacks in class. My heart would pound and I would sweat uncontrollably. No matter how many showers I took or how much deodorant I used, Calculus left my T-shirt soaking, and me smelling like a goat. I started to pack an extra shirt in my backpack.

Calculus anxiety followed me into bed. I would lie there hugging my dad's old sweater, running through problems in my head, making more and more mistakes in my panic. I've never been particularly athletic or musical. Being smart was the one thing I had going for me. *If I wasn't getting good grades, what the hell was I worth? What was I doing? What would happen to me?* My thoughts ran in circles and I couldn't stop them.

I would sweat uncontrollably

I didn't know that the worst was yet to come. My mom happened to be out of town when my brother woke up to the smell of smoke in his room. It was a Sunday morning in early March, still pitch dark. My sister was up, wrapped in a towel, getting ready for work. Her screams jolted me awake. By then the fire was four feet up the wall. I frantically searched my brother's room, looking for our elderly cat. When I found her, half her whiskers were singed off. She protested when I crammed her into my backpack on top of the books. My sister and brother each grabbed a dog by the collar. We all ran barefoot across the icy lawn.

A minute later the TV in my brother's room exploded. We stood on the sidewalk, mouths open, watching the house burn, while our neighbors called the fire department. From the safety of their living room, we could hear the windows in our house popping. Then I remembered! My dad's jersey and sweater were in my bedroom closet. I ran outside and back toward the house. A fireman grabbed me and shouted, "Is somebody still in there?" I shook my head and started sobbing. My sister came after me and wrapped me in her arms. We lost all our stuff, everything in our bedrooms. All I had were the pajamas I was wearing and the books in my backpack. Later, while the firemen sprayed a chemical foam onto our roof, I sat at the neighbors' dining room table with the dogs and the cat at my feet. I had my textbook open, trying to study for my calculus test the next day. My sister came in and asked, "What are you doing? Your teacher will let you off. Just chill!"

I was afraid to change anything

I said, "No! I have to do well on this test!"

She took the book away from me. "Calm down," she said. "Just sit on the couch for a minute." She made me some tea, but my hands were shaking so much I couldn't hold the mug. I'd already lost my dad and now I'd nearly lost my little brother. I remember thinking, *This stuff doesn't happen to people! People don't lose their dad and then have their house burn down! It just doesn't happen. It's ridiculous!*

After that, my worrying stopped being specific. It became a heavy yellow cloud that followed me around. I was afraid to change anything, hanging on to my old routines for dear life. I walked the same route to school every day. I wore the same pair of shoes. I ate the same cheese sandwich for lunch. But then one day Meggie invited me to join a bunch of kids for pizza and simply wouldn't take no for an answer. She grabbed my hand and physically pulled me after her.

Recovery

Meggie's hand forced my moment of truth. I realized that my anxiety was hurting me as much as those scissors once did. It took a while but I finally started dealing with it. Slowly, bit by bit, the yellow cloud shrank. I may never be a happy-go-lucky person, but now when I feel that terrible heaviness, I know what to do.

For me, one specific thing wasn't the answer; it was a combination of things. Talking to the school social worker helped. I started seeing her every week. I also got busy, doing things that made me happy. I joined a bunch of clubs at school and wrote and directed a play. Writing turned out to be a great way to relieve my pain.

I still feel the sadness sometimes. Father's Day is worse than the anniversary of my dad's death. No one is talking about how awesome it is to have a dad in July. I started to learn to deal internally with what I could, and to outwardly express what I couldn't.

When our cat went into kidney failure, my panic swept back in like a tidal wave. But this time I wrote away my fear and sadness, in long, stream-of-consciousness passages. When I was finished, I lay on the floor and let my chest feel heavy, as if it were anchoring me.

The writing had emptied my mind and I stared up at the ceiling, not thinking, just feeling. I felt all the grief and pain and anxiety and loneliness and anger, and then I let them drift away. I thought about the cat, and our old house, and my dad, and calculated whether the joy of having had them outweighed the sadness of losing them. I knew the answer was yes.

I
was
raw meat
to bullies

Exiled

ALANA

Always the outsider. That was me. It was terrifying.

It didn't start out that way. I was an outgoing, happy little kid. I'm the oldest of four: two girls and two boys. We're a really tight family. It's part of our Spanish culture. Our tiny Manhattan apartment was always full of friends and music and the smell of spicy food. There's a video of me at about three years old, grinning from ear to ear as I danced to merengue on the boom box.

My mom and dad both grew up poor; she's from Cuba and he's from El Salvador. They never had the opportunity to go to college and they wanted something more for their kids. When I was six, we moved out of New York City in search of a better life.

We settled in a small city in New Jersey, but it was hard finding an affordable apartment on a safe street. There was a lot of crime on our block: drug deals were common and sometimes there were shootings. But none of this prepared me for the trials ahead.

Perfect target

My parents had drummed into us that we should make something of ourselves. They saw their brothers and sisters trapped in hopelessness by lousy jobs or no jobs at all, and they didn't want that for their kids. Neither did I. No one in my family had ever gone to college, and I was the one who was going to change that. I don't know where I got the idea that I wanted to be a lawyer. I didn't actually know any lawyers, but I had it all figured out: I was going to do well in school so I could get a scholarship and when I became a lawyer, I could take care of my whole family.

I was horribly self-conscious

I couldn't wait to graduate from sixth grade because it brought the future one step closer. But middle school turned out to be a horrible place. The building was old and dark, with chipped and wobbly desks and rusty lockers that screeched when you opened them. The bathrooms were painted black and had patches of reeking mold.

Many of the kids, like me, had moved from New York, but they had brought their big-city problems with them. The smell of weed wafted at every school entrance. Kids showed up to class drunk. Nearly every week there was a violent fight. The teachers were worn down: the students dissed them and called them names.

I stuck out like a sore thumb. It seemed like I was the only kid who took books out of the library or asked questions in class or handed my homework in on time. To make matters worse, I might have come straight from central casting as "the kid to pick on." I wore glasses and braces and was twenty pounds pudgier than most of the other girls. And yet when they started to fill out in seventh and eighth grade, I stayed flat. At lunch, kids called me "tabletop tits" and "orangutan titties." I was horribly self-conscious.

Even if I could have afforded the stuff other girls wore, I hated what I thought of as the stereotype of a Latina. I didn't want to be the half-naked girl you see in music videos. But that's what the girls in my grade were after, the clothing brands advertised by rappers and hip-hop singers and pop stars. They wanted boyfriends and sex and alcohol and drugs. I didn't want those things and it was obvious, so I was raw meat to bullies.

Mean girls

Girls usually started the bullying, and if boys were there, they would join in. The name-calling went from "You're fat. You're a nerd. You're a dork" to "You're a disgrace to your culture."

I was never physically hurt by a guy, but their words were like knife wounds. "You're so ugly no one will ever want to be with you," they said. "You don't do justice to being Latina."

I was afraid of the boys' words, but I was more afraid of the girls' fists. When I was thirteen, girls would beat me up after school. They would throw me against the lockers, break open my locker, and steal my stuff. I was especially scared of the bathroom, where they would ambush me, pulling my hair and shoving my head into the toilet.

I planned when I would go to pee. I would try to go twice before I left home, or make sure I timed it for during a class. I would crack open the bathroom door and see if anyone was in there before I dared to go in. If I had a bad feeling, I would just hold it.

The mean girls knew how to find me. It was beyond scary. Everything in your body sinks down. It's like being on a roller coaster with that feeling in the pit of your stomach. "Why'd you even come to school today?" they'd taunt. "You knew this was going to happen."

I tried to stay calm because running away just made things worse. Whatever I did, they made it my fault. For two years I didn't have a single friend. I ate lunch by myself every day. I went to school hoping I could get through the day without having to call a security guard or ending up at the hospital.

Bad dreams

At home I pretended everything was fine but the torment haunted me in my sleep.

> I ate lunch by myself every day

I had nightmares of being trapped in a dark corner, people engulfing me, cold hands grasping my ankles. I'd wake up in the middle of the night gasping for breath.

My mom called the school to report the students who were harassing me, but the principal and teachers said without proof there was nothing they could do. The bullying killed the friendly, outgoing kid I used to be. I wasn't ever genuinely happy.

My mom saw that and it broke her heart. Many times I heard her crying.

Then my mom did two amazing things for me. She found me a psychologist so I'd have someone to confide in. And the summer after eighth grade, Mom enrolled me in a theater program where I met kids from other schools. They treated me like I was worth their time. They helped me open up and be myself again. The director of the program saw something in me. "You're really talented," he said. "You should apply for a scholarship at the school where I work." This was a private high school a half hour from where I lived.

Too good to be true

My mom did two amazing things for me

The school's tuition was ridiculously high: $24,000 a year. That was more than my dad made in a year. He and my mom were unsure about the school, but they let me apply for the scholarship. I wrote an essay about my life in middle school. The director of the school called and offered me a full ride for four years. I was ecstatic.

The new school was the most beautiful place I had ever seen. It looked like a college campus, with solid redbrick buildings, velvety green lawns, old shady trees, and benches that beckoned you to spend the afternoon in the sunshine.

It couldn't have been more different from my old school, but I was still an exile. For one thing, nearly everyone else was white. They'd been friends since kindergarten. They were rich. All their lives, they'd had good teachers, plenty of books, and all kinds of support. Now, instead of being the girl who couldn't fit in because she was a homely brain, I was the dumb Latina who couldn't keep up and had no friends. It didn't matter that the reasons were different: I was at the bottom of the heap. Again.

I tried hard to fit in. I was cheerful and chatty. I joined the tennis team (even though I sat on the bench). I changed my outfits from flowery prints and jeans to bright polos and khakis. But when people were friendly to me it felt fake. It was like, *I'm going to be nice to you so I don't seem like a racist jerk.*

The stress was taking its toll. The laughing kid in our home videos was long gone. I chewed my nails until my fingers bled. I could fall asleep but only for a couple of hours. Then I'd jerk awake and lie there running through the list of things that I hated about myself. When I cried, I pressed my pillow against my face so that nobody would hear. I didn't think much about being a lawyer anymore. I couldn't stand my life.

My only relief was music. I sang a lot. Alone in my room, I would belt out songs from Broadway musicals. My favorites were the down-and-out songs, about people like me who felt different or not good enough.

I couldn't let my parents know how bad it really was because I didn't want them to worry again, or to feel like they were paying for me to get ridiculed. They had spent so much for this school. Yes, tuition was free, but gas, food, and course fees cost us about $1,500 per year. My dad's a collision expert and he worked overtime in the body shop to make ends meet. He could fix anything, but not my busted-up life.

My suffering was a secret: I wanted my pain to be *my* pain, not to inflict it on anybody else. *I hate everyone*, I often thought. But most of the time, my thoughts were more brutal. *I hate myself! Why was I born this way?*

Rescue

One morning I was having a particularly hard time. I don't even remember the comment somebody made, but it put me over the edge and I headed straight for Mr. Guthrie's office. It was almost a reflex to go there when I felt bad. He was the drama teacher and my new guidance counselor. I walked in and swept the old tin toys he kept on his desk to the floor. Then I burst into tears.

"I can't stand it for one more minute! No one cares about me!" I wailed. "No matter where I go, there's no place for me. I don't know what I did to deserve this!"

It was 11:00 in the morning. Mr. Guthrie canceled all his classes and meetings for the day. "Listen," he said. "We're going to sit here and talk about everything that you're feeling and everything that's happened to make you feel this way."

He had opened a tap. Everything gushed out. I told him about middle school. I told him the name of every person who had ever hurt me, and what they had done or said. The lunch bell rang, and then afternoon classes began. I talked for three hours.

When I finally stopped, Mr. Guthrie asked if I wanted to get something to eat. We sat at a café and he told me what it had been like for him, growing up without parents. He talked about how hard it was for him to live his life. He wanted to study theater and people made fun of him. The guys-can't-do-theater thing. He told me that when he was a newcomer at this school, none of the faculty had accepted him at first. They treated him just like the kids treated me.

"But you always seem so happy," I said. "You never seem upset."

"I've seen enough of people's ignorance to know that it's not worth my time," he said. "I'm only as good as I make myself out to be. Just because people have opinions doesn't make them true. All that is important is how I see myself, knowing where I want to go and what I want to do."

When I'd heard things like that before, they'd sounded so clichéd. In that moment, they felt true. And that's all he said. No big speech. No fireworks going off in my head.

On the way back to school, we listened to the sound track of *Carousel*, the musical we were going to put on that year. That was all that happened. I hadn't needed someone to tell me I was beautiful or smart. I just needed someone to be there, to say *I care* without even saying it. I realized then that it wasn't what Mr. Guthrie said or how he said it. It was that he took the time to listen to me. I'd never had anyone do that other than my parents. I love them to death; they did everything they could for me. But I needed that caring and reassurance from someone outside my family, too.

Things didn't change overnight

I was lucky that Mr. Guthrie was there. If anybody reading this thinks, *That's fine, but there's no Mr. Guthrie for me*, all I can say is, you just have to find one.

Learning to value myself

From then on I was more confident. Things didn't change overnight. Lots of kids still ignored me but I picked myself up and decided it didn't matter. I freed myself from constantly measuring my level of misery. As I became less anxious and depressed, I found it easier to make friends. I got parts in musicals and plays and met new people through those shows. By the end of sophomore year, I had a solid group of friends.

By the next year I'd gone from being "that Spanish girl who got a scholarship" to "Lani, the girl who's funny and good at singing and acting." Girls even invited me to their slumber parties. It seemed that all my friends had been to fifty of them, but I had never been to a single one. The first time I was, like, crying. I couldn't believe I'd been invited! It was awesome.

It takes a long time to find out who we are. I had spent so many years letting other people define me that I didn't have a chance to appreciate myself. I learned to value how compassionate and caring I am. I learned to appreciate how much I have going for me—my intelligence and my performing talents. I realized that even though bad things had happened to me, I was not a bad person.

My anxieties and insecurities and other people don't define me. Only *I* get to do that.

I couldn't get the idea out of my mind: a dog rushing at me and no way to escape

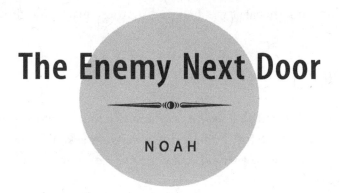

The Enemy Next Door

NOAH

If you dropped in from an exoplanet, you might think I was one of the lucky ones. I grew up in a rambling house with a truckload of electronics and a saltwater pool in the backyard. I played drums and was one of the stars on the town swim team. Not a care in the world, right? Wrong.

For as long as I can remember, I've had a source of anxiety that stabs me like a poisoned dart: cynophobia. Sound exotic? I wish it were. Cynophobia means "fear of dogs." Any hint of a dog—a smell, a sound—and I'd feel gripped by panic inside. It didn't matter if the dog was no bigger than a catcher's mitt and belonged to the harmless old lady down the street.

There are all kinds of phobias. People can be afraid of snakes, heights, blood, and even clowns. No phobia is fun, but some triggers are easier to avoid than others. If you're afraid of flying, you can decide you won't fly.

It's almost impossible to avoid dogs. Every time I left home, I knew I might see one: Big, hulking ones with faces like squashed trolls. Little ones with pointy ears and earsplitting barks. They all set me off. I didn't want to be nuzzled or licked or slobbered on, but mostly I didn't want to get bitten. Everyone thinks that *their* dog is friendly. But I knew better: at any moment, catastrophe could strike. Sharp teeth clamping down on my hand, claws impaling my throat. I was haunted by these gruesome thoughts.

Going to the dogs

Friends who had dogs were another problem. Before going to someone's house for the first time, I always asked if there was a dog. If there was, I would make an excuse or invite him to my house instead.

One time I forgot to ask. A kid named Kyle had joined the swim team. We became friends and I was happy when he invited me to his birthday party. But when I rang the doorbell, I heard a dog barking its head off. I turned into a block of ice.

Kyle's mom answered the door, holding on to the collar of a big yellow dog.

"I don't like dogs," I said as calmly as I could. I was fighting the impulse to run. "Do you think you could keep it in another room?"

"Don't worry. Juno won't hurt you," she told me. "We have to let her loose or she'll bark even more." She smiled and let go of Juno's collar. I dropped Kyle's present and ran down the sidewalk.

She shouted, "Don't run! Don't run! She thinks you're playing!" I heard the jangle of Juno's collar as she bounded after me. The next thing I knew, Kyle was bellowing, "Here, Juno, get your treat!" Juno turned around and trotted home.

That was the last time I ever went to Kyle's.

My parents considered getting a dog as a way of easing me out of my phobia. My older sister would have been overjoyed. But my dad was not into the idea of having his stuff wrecked

by a teething puppy. My parents suggested that I see a doctor, but I resisted—even though I knew this phobia was messing with my life.

In middle school I got all my closest friends to swear they'd sacrifice their lives to protect me from a dog. My best friend, Jack, had two border collies. He lived in a pretty small house and his family was really careful about keeping the dogs locked up when I came over.

Tough love was not the answer

But not everyone showed that kind of allegiance. Another friend's mom decided a tough-love approach would liberate me. There I was, hanging out with her son after a baseball game, trying to be cool. She showed up with her little dog and it made a beeline for me.

As my friend watched, she egged on the dog until it started running circles around me right there in the parking lot. "A big strapping boy like you," she said. (I was nearly six feet.) "You can't be afraid of this teensy pup." It was humiliating. I hated her for doing that. I didn't blame people for having dogs, but if you rubbed your dog in my face, we were done.

After the scene at the ballpark, I tried to keep my fears to myself. I found a longer way home from school so I could avoid all the neighborhood dogs. Don't get the idea I was a wimp—not with people. Still, I was relieved when in high school everyone seemed to have forgotten about my dog thing.

But why did I have this phobia? No dog had bitten me when I was a kid. My sister definitely didn't share my fear. She would have traded me in for a cocker spaniel any day. A doctor once told me to think of it as a holdover from prehistoric times, an instinctive defense against becoming prey. An interesting theory, maybe, but it didn't help me much. My mom had had the same fear of dogs as a child, so maybe it was genetic. Lucky Mom: she had simply outgrown her childhood fear. I would have loved to wake up one day and not have to worry about it anymore. I wanted to relax and enjoy myself, and I knew my fear was unreasonable, but I couldn't control my thoughts. I gave up trying to figure out where my phobia came from.

Anxiety did not fit my cool-guy style

Being anxious was not my style. I'm actually pretty laid-back. I have long hair. I think of myself as a cool guy. What with the drums, a shelf full of swimming medals, and my sense of humor, I was one of the popular kids. But inside me was that poisoned dart that never let me relax.

One day my mom came home with a story that freaked me out. She was walking in a nature preserve close to our house when a Doberman came running at her, unleashed. She said loudly, "Please call off your dog." Luckily the owner was right there and he stopped the dog. I realized that I would not have been able to handle it as calmly as she did, not even close. I would have gone into full-blown panic mode. Afterward I couldn't get the idea out of my mind: a dog rushing at me and no way to escape. I kept asking myself, *Where would I run? How could I get away?* It really put a cramp in my style, and things came to a head one Saturday in June.

The height of panic

> I sat on the gravel, wishing I were dead

It was the opening of the swim season at a quarry about a half hour from town, and we'd planned a fund-raiser for the team. There'd be demonstrations and races, followed by a barbecue. I was looking forward to the break from final exams.

I was one of the last people to be picked up by the bus. There was an empty seat near the front. My friend Lila was in the next seat, and we started talking. About five minutes later, we heard a yelp from the back of the bus. I quickly turned around and saw a huge black Newfoundland on the backseat. I froze.

Lila said, "The coach thought it would be fun to have his dog do a mock rescue. That's what he's bred for ..."

She was still talking when I lunged across her and pulled the emergency break.

"Stop the bus, I'm going to be sick," I yelled to the driver. It wasn't a lie. I felt ready to barf. I scrambled out the door and practically fell onto the side of the road.

I wouldn't get back into the bus. Lila tried coaxing me. Then the kids got upset because we were going to miss the opening race. I told the driver I would walk home. "Can't let you do that, son," he said. We were all stuck. I sat on the gravel next to the bus, waiting for my dad to pick me up, wishing I were dead. Needless to say, I missed the whole event and made everyone else late. I wasn't surprised that people were mad at me. I was furious with myself.

The enemy waits

We were sitting down for dinner after the last day of school when my parents said they had something to tell us.

"Guess what? We're going to the south of France for vacation!" my mom said. That was good news. "We're staying at a country hotel," she went on.

"It's perfect," my dad chimed in. "Really beautiful, with great food."

I could see from their expressions there was more to it. The "but" was dogs. There were five of them.

My hands got clammy and I felt my throat catch. So much for a relaxing vacation.

"Talk to the owners and see if they can keep them away from me," I said bravely, knowing from bitter experience that even the best intentions go awry.

> I resigned myself to the inevitable

I considered causing a big fuss and refusing to go. But that would have disappointed everyone, and I didn't want a repeat of the bus fiasco. So I resigned myself to the inevitable. On the train down to southern France, I rehearsed what might happen and how I might protect myself: I could jump on top of a car. I could climb a tree.

The minute we got there, the adrenaline started pumping and I could feel my hands tremble. Five dogs greeted us. All shapes and sizes, they walked around like they owned the place. Impossible to escape.

"Great," I said under my breath.

But it was also impossible to resist the laid-back vibe of the place. The gardens, the views, the quiet walks—if ever there was a place to chill, this was it. I had a pile of books with me and found great places to hide away and read.

For some reason, one of the dogs really loved hanging out with me. It would trot after me and keep me company, stretched out in the sun. One of the other dogs liked to join us. Don't ask me what kind they were. One had floppy ears, the other was fuzzy. A third dog was more hesitant and would stay put for a really long time; no surprise moves with that one. Sometimes the dogs would get up slowly and amble away. I liked that. I started to relax around them.

The enemy retreats—on my terms

That summer was the turning point for me. I never thought I would get over my anxiety, but I did. Now I can be around dogs and it's no problem. It was exposure on my own terms that made the difference. When we got home, a psychologist friend of my parents told us that phobias can be overcome in just this way. Other people had tried to *make* me like dogs. When I came to know them slowly, by myself, it was fine.

Getting older also helped. I realized I had greater control over my thoughts than when I was younger. *This dog is not going to rip my head off*, I could reason. *It's not the wolf in* The Three Little Pigs.

I may never have a dog of my own. But at least I don't run from them anymore. I've come to enjoy a wagging tail.

Count Me Out

BRIONY

A photo of four Victorian ladies in their satiny best sits on the mantelpiece in our dining room. The one on the right, Aunt Emily, is the one I look like. Family lore has it that she was too fragile to go into society. The slightest excitement gave her "the vapors." Emily lived like that for ninety-five years. It could have been her tight corset, but I think that she suffered from anxiety.

It's in my genes

Anxiety runs in our family. You see it in my mother when she asks a million questions before she buys anything. I sound just like her when I take ten minutes to choose an ice cream flavor. My dad has chronic insomnia, a sign of anxiety that's easy to hide from the outside world.

I was a teenager before I realized that I'd inherited some of my parents' constant worry, along with their love of reading and jazz. It's not as if it showed up out of nowhere at age fourteen:

I just hadn't noticed the connection. The trigger for my anxiety was as humdrum as one, two, three: I couldn't make sense of numbers.

Because I'd started reading so early, my parents sent me to a school for gifted kids. I *was* above average in lots of ways: I could recite poetry and speak Spanish and play the piano. It didn't occur to anybody that I wouldn't catch on to math sooner or later. But I never did. Math facts, measuring, manipulating numbers, spatial relationships—they were all like some crazy code to me.

Odd one out

By the time I hit high school, I had full-blown number anxiety. This showed up in peculiar ways. I was terrified, of all things, of using my locker. Related to my math woes was confusion about left and right. A combination lock with all those turns and numbers made me break into a sweat.

So I didn't use my locker and instead just lugged all my stuff around with me until my mother came up with this simple trick: instead of right and left, I did thumb up, thumb down.

I could never escape the feeling of being *different* from everybody else. I was the only one I knew who spent half her time in advanced literature, language, and history classes, and the other half in remedial math and science. Just about everybody in my advanced classes was college-bound, some headed to Harvard or MIT. In my remedial classes, it was either community college or a minimum-wage job. I lost nights of sleep worrying about how I'd stack up in the college sweepstakes. No matter how good I was in English and history, math and science would drag me down. This feeling of being "less than" never really went away.

My anxiety about numbers wasn't confined to the classroom.

Bus schedules made me crazy; it was like they were written in hieroglyphics. I got mixed up and would stand at the bus stop for ages. That's when my mind would really spin out of control: *What if the bus isn't coming? I could freeze to death!*

I had a part-time job at an organic deli where my parents had been customers for years. I was okay when I was behind the counter making tofu-avocado wraps. My problem was the bulk-food bins. They were math hell. The owner was kind and never lost patience with me, but no matter how many times I weighed customers' bags of oats and flaxseed, I was never sure I'd got it right.

It got so that I felt waves of anxiety just walking in the door. I became terrified I'd have a full-blown panic attack during my shift. That's when I knew it was time to quit. Another failure.

Stress 101: learning to drive was torture

I've read about vision quests, a rite of passage where teenagers in some Native American cultures go alone into the wilderness and fast for many days. I would happily have traded places with any of them: our local rite of passage was learning how to drive. Kids didn't judge each other so much by the clothes they wore—it was more about the cars they drove. Pretty much everybody's social life in high school was wrapped up in car culture: owning one, fixing one, driving one. And driving, of course, means navigating traffic and judging how wide to take a turn. I dreaded it. Give me darkness and deprivation any day!

I took a driving-education class in my junior year along with everyone else. It was an awful experience. The teacher that year was borderline sadistic. He loved to use scare tactics, doing things like showing us a video about people who died in car accidents because they weren't wearing seat belts. All I remember are images of bloody, broken bodies and gore-smeared windshields.

I couldn't get those pictures out of my head when I was learning to drive my parents' car. I was sick with fear, and every minute I thought I was going to die. Either Mom or Dad was always calling out "Keep left!" or "Merge on your right," and that just made me panic. So I taped signs that said *left* and *right* on either side of the steering wheel. It was worse when they shouted, "Watch out for the parked cars!"

I had trouble judging distances, so it was hard for me to tell how far I was from the curb or a stop sign or oncoming cars. I did finally get my license, but I sure wasn't anyone's first choice for a ride.

I just didn't fit in

Not that it mattered. I usually had nowhere to go and no one to go with. In the social swirl of high school, I barely existed. It wasn't that the other kids were unfriendly. I just didn't fit in; I didn't belong. Maybe I was too tall, or too serious, or maybe the other kids could sense my unease.

Imagine how excited I felt toward the end of my junior year, when I was invited to a party on the other side of the city. Josh, a guy who lived down the street, offered me a ride. I changed my clothes about ten times, then my parents grilled me about who else was going, whether the parents would be home, what we would be doing, whether there would be nourishing food or just jun ... I fudged the answers because I didn't really know. For some reason, they didn't ask about alcohol, but there turned out to be plenty of that.

By the time the host kid's parents came home, I was about the only one who was sober. Josh tossed me his car keys and held the door open for a bunch of other kids who wanted a sober ride. They were looking to *me* to save the day.

Firmly, I took the steering wheel and ordered everybody to put on seat belts. That's when I realized that the signs I had taped in our car weren't going to do me much good in this one. I drove cautiously, taking one turn so wide that I nearly wiped out cars parked on the other side of the street. The other kids hooted. Then the outline of a gas pump appeared among the dials on the dashboard. I knew that meant we were getting low. "How many miles does it say we have?" mumbled Josh.

I couldn't read the number with confidence so I took a guess. "Um, fifty."

"That's plenty," he said, nodding off.

I had guessed wrong. Then I got lost. I couldn't read the street signs in the dark and had no idea which direction was which. Twenty miles later, we ran out of gas on a busy road, cars honking and swerving to avoid us. The kids swore at me as they woke up. Finally, Josh came to and went in search of a gas station. By the time he got back with some fuel in a can, he'd sobered up and abruptly told me he'd drive home. My whole body turned hot with shame. I felt cast aside and inadequate.

Finding release

As I lay in bed, I relived every excruciating moment of the evening, making myself more and more anxious. The next morning I felt cut off and alone. I could barely throw off the blankets and get up. All day I felt exhausted and on the verge of tears. I dreaded going back to school on Monday. The idea of it made me so fidgety I wanted to jump out of my skin. That was one of my all-time lowest moments.

I look back at that time and wonder how I stood it. How did I get from that sad place to a college dorm where I'm actually enjoying the chance to go to class?

The one thing that freed me from anxiety in high school was poetry. I had always loved to read it and I gradually learned how to write it. That fall I did an independent poetry study with a really good teacher. He was smart and supportive and gave me great advice about my poems. I loved working at something

I could master and I even won an award. More than anything else, defining myself as a poet helped me survive the rest of high school. By saying *This is what I do*, the numbers curse and my lack of friends didn't seem as painful.

Finding relief

Another huge help was getting testing to figure out why I had two different brains in one body. The results weren't great but they cheered me up. I was officially diagnosed with a learning disability called dyscalculia, like dyslexia for math. It was a relief to finally put a name to something I had struggled with my whole life. At first I wondered, *Is it real? Why has nobody ever heard of it?* Well, it turns out to be quite common but under the radar in a lot of people. I wasn't such a misfit after all.

Getting rid of my guilt was a big step

After I was diagnosed, I agreed to see a psychotherapist. It was incredibly helpful to have someone to talk to about all the really hard stuff without feeling self-pitying or like I was a burden. It also gave me space to work out why I felt so bad and to come up with ways to feel better. In hindsight, I wish I'd done it much earlier.

Until I was diagnosed, there was always a voice in my head, *If I just try harder, I'll learn*. Getting rid of my guilt was a big step. I found a math tutor who was a fantastic teacher and a true friend. She helped me beyond the classroom, suggesting that I keep a list of the times when I felt really bad. "When you see a pattern," she advised, "stay away from that person or that situation. There are some things you have to face, but there's no point sweating stuff that you can easily avoid." That was hard to do in high school but it's easier now, in college, where I have more control. I can recognize those potential triggers and steer clear.

Once I started to talk about being anxious, the floodgates opened. For the first time in my life, I felt secure enough to make friends with a couple of other kids who were dealing with anxiety. I had always assumed that they had it all together, and they had thought the same about me! We discovered that we each had our own strategies for managing anxiety. My strategies weren't always the right answer for them, and vice versa, but it helped us to share our ways of coping.

I made a pact with myself: once I graduated, I'd never, ever take another math class. With a bit of effort, I found a college with no course requirements. Now I'm able to concentrate on literature and history, subjects that make me light up. My transition to the bigger world was actually easy. I still have my struggles with anxiety, but it doesn't dominate my life anymore.

I'm still hopeless at numbers, but I've found ways to cope. If I need to do mental math, I make sure I have some time and a quiet place to do it; for basic monetary transactions, like grocery shopping on a budget or leaving a tip, I bring a calculator. Navigating directions is still very challenging. When finding my way to a new place, I always allow extra time and print out written directions ahead of time. I'm also better at asking for help now than I used to be.

I don't write much poetry these days, but I still tend to think in metaphors. In high school I was flying lower than everyone else because I was dragging a huge, invisible weight. In college, the weight is gone. Suddenly I can soar.

I
lived
in terror
of negative
judgments

Stuck

GITA

I'd been thinking all week about the first school dance of my seventh-grade year. But I still didn't know if I was going to go. Making decisions was my idea of a nightmare.

"Do you think I should go to the dance?" I asked my parents for the umpteenth time. We all knew what was coming next.

"It's up to you, Gita," said my mother, trying to keep an even keel.

"What do *you* think of the dance?" I persisted. "If I don't go, will I miss out on everything?"

"Stop asking the same questions!" my father said. "How many times do we have to answer you?"

"If you want to go, go!" said my mother, her voice getting shrill.

I drove my parents crazy when I tied myself into mental knots. They didn't understand the deeper issue behind the questions. I didn't either.

The day of the dance finally came, and the start time was closing in. Suddenly I knew I should go and I begged my father

40 ➤ FREAKING OUT

to give me a ride. Halfway there, I changed my mind; I wanted to stay home after all. He slammed on the brakes and lurched the car into a U-turn, berating me for wasting his time.

If I hadn't been able to hear, walk, or breathe on my own, it would have been obvious that I needed help. But when I was growing up, no one saw that I was suffering. My parents didn't know or didn't want to know. Later, I learned that my behavior was just one symptom of the anxiety that was consuming my life.

Urgent urges

As a little girl, I was afraid to express my feelings to my parents for fear they would criticize me. I lived in terror of negative judgments. I soothed myself by touching and counting the pieces of Lego in 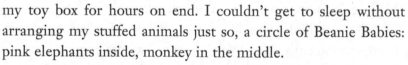 my toy box for hours on end. I couldn't get to sleep without arranging my stuffed animals just so, a circle of Beanie Babies: pink elephants inside, monkey in the middle.

I didn't exactly outgrow those rituals; I just traded them in for others. I brushed my hair exactly one hundred times and my teeth for exactly two minutes. When I finished reading, I made sure that the book was lined up with the corners of my bedside table. Things on angles made me feel funny.

At first I liked school because it was one long routine. I liked the lineups and the bells, the stacks of paper and the lessons that followed one another, always in the same order. But I dreaded speaking in class. Those seconds waiting to see whose name the teacher would call filled me with terror. Even when I knew the answer, the words didn't come out right; I couldn't seem to make myself clear. My deepest fear was that someone would put me down or laugh at me.

Only my stuff made me feel safe. My mom harangued me about the things I kept in my room, piles and piles of it. Old school assignments, clothes that didn't fit, stacks of newspapers, recipes, and horoscopes, even empty boxes, all arranged in rows. I hated when I had to clean my room. I would sit on the bed sorting through the piles for hours because I agonized over what to keep and what to throw away. Getting rid of anything made me sad and anxious.

Stigma and shame

I didn't know that I had an anxiety disorder. I had no idea there were other people out there going through the same things I was.

It's not that my parents weren't attentive. Far from it. They were traditional Indian parents, and they wanted to raise us the same way they had been raised. My dad dictated everything we did, from when we ate to what we watched on TV. He even opened our mail. My mom enforced a strict curfew. Being a girl, I was never allowed out after dark, and in the winter I had to be home by five o'clock. Mom hadn't been allowed to go out at night as a girl, so why should I? I never once had a sleepover. I never went trick-or-treating. My friend Carrie's birthday was on Halloween and she always invited me to go out with her. My parents said no.

My parents had moved to Vancouver before my brother and I were born, and they'd had a hard time. My dad was an engineer in India, but the only job he could get here was driving a cab. My mother was a surgeon and was now working as a cashier until she could take the exams to qualify in Canada. They rarely socialized and never really felt at ease in their adopted country. Having children only increased their fears. They worried about all the crime they saw on TV. Maybe they felt they had to control us in order to protect us.

One thing's for sure: they wanted me to be a perfect child. My older brother has autism and the supposed shame of this was something they lived with every day. My parents attach a strong stigma to mental illness and don't like anyone to talk about, or even know about, my brother. My parents couldn't tolerate the idea that there was something wrong with me, too.

Am I really that weird?

Despite all my odd behavior, I am actually outgoing and funny. I've had the same close friends since kindergarten.

I didn't know my compulsions were unusual until, when I was ten, I went to a wedding where there were six hundred guests. The ladies' bathroom was a mob scene. Several women were waiting behind me to get to the mirror to fix their makeup. I tried to ignore them as I washed and rewashed my hands. One of the women said, "Enough already! You're going to rub your hands away!" Everybody clucked their disapproval but I couldn't make myself stop. Someone had to yank me away from the sink.

After that, my rituals started to get in the way of my life. It was a double whammy: what I called my routines (actually compulsions) were taking up more and more of my time so I was seeing my three friends less often. It wasn't just that. My rituals embarrassed me. I wanted to hide them.

I was secretive and ashamed

By the time I got to high school, I was secretive and ashamed. I began to avoid all kinds of situations I should have loved. It took a lot of effort for me to try out for a singing role in the spring musical, *Oliver!* I have a good voice, and getting a part should have been a breeze. The music coach made a big deal of telling us that she was running the audition like a professional production. She expected us to learn our parts, practice, and be on time.

I was more nervous about it than I realized. I laid out my clothes the night before, as I always did, but when I got up, they didn't seem quite right. I changed my mind about the red shirt I had chosen but the blue shirt wasn't a great color on me. Besides, I was supposed to be dressed like an English street urchin. I found an old cotton dress that seemed dowdy enough but it had a stain.

I began to fret, and to sweat. I was putting on clothes and tearing them off while the minutes ticked by. I missed my bus, of course, and by the time I got to school, the auditions were almost over.

My distress signal got cut off

I could tell that the coach was furious. I had only sung a few lines when she put up her hand. "Okay!" she said, meaning, *Go sit down*. It was humiliating. The room was dead quiet. No one even clapped. I felt my face burning. I had ruined the audition by being late.

The next day, my homeroom teacher caught me counting the lockers in the hall between classes. At the end of the day, she called me into her classroom. She was the one high school teacher who'd actually taken an interest in me. I confided that I was sad and couldn't think straight anymore. When she heard this, she got the school social worker involved. The social worker asked if I'd like to get together before class in a few days. We arranged to meet in front of the gym. When I arrived, she wasn't there. I couldn't understand why, and my teacher never mentioned it again. After that I gave up.

I only found out much later that the teacher had called my mom, and my mom had talked to the social worker. Mom convinced her that she was doing a good job of raising me and that I was fine. My distress signal got cut off. Nobody heard the alarm.

I am still mad at my mother about that call. But I honestly think she had no idea how desperate I was. That's because I did a good job of hiding it. Maybe she was too caught up in her unhappiness: taking care of my brother had put her own plans on hold. In our family we don't really talk about our feelings, so they're kind of invisible.

My world grew smaller and smaller. I'd go home, study, and spend a couple of hours brushing my hair, brushing my teeth, washing my hands, and then starting all over again before it was time for bed.

I'm lucky my friends didn't bail on me. At lunch I hung out with three girls, each of us a funny misfit in our own way. I liked to laugh, and Carrie told great jokes. Helena was a fantastic mimic, and Lianne saw real life as one hilarious sitcom. Somehow we all missed out on the elusive popularity gene.

It's weird, but for a long time I didn't realize that Carrie wore a wig. Even when I did know about it, I never asked her why. It was as if we had an unspoken pact not to invade each other's space or make emotional demands. Others weren't as understanding.

Theo was a kid we all avoided because he was mean to the bone. At lunch one day he pulled Carrie's wig off and paraded it around the cafeteria. People had no clue what to make of the tufts of blond hair on her nearly bald scalp.

Theo was expelled, and for a while everyone was super nice to Carrie. We all assumed that she had cancer. A week or so later, Carrie texted that she wanted to come over. I was worried that she'd stay too long and put me off my schedule, so I took her into the living room instead of my room. We sat on the sofa slurping tea and eating samosas. Carrie took off her hat. I tried not to stare at her head.

"You're probably wondering what's wrong with me," she said.
"Of course I am! I'm worried about you. Do you have cancer?"
"I have OCD."
She explained that she had obsessive-compulsive disorder,

and it took the form of pulling out her hair. It had started in middle school with her eyebrows. I noticed that they were almost gone. She said she couldn't stop herself; it was like an addiction.

As she told me more about OCD, something started to click for me. I realized that there might be a name for what was wrong with me.

Dark days

You might assume that I went and got help right away, but I didn't. I wasn't ready to give up my routines, or have anyone make me try. Even the thought of it made my compulsions worse. I managed to get up and go to school each morning, but I started wearing the same navy-blue outfit day in and day out. In my third year of high school, I couldn't concentrate anymore. Maybe I was worn out from battling all those compulsions I didn't understand. That winter I struggled with suicidal thoughts. For the first time, I wasn't on the honor roll.

Carrie knew something was wrong. She asked me about it, but I couldn't explain. It was so frustrating—I really had no idea how to describe how I felt. It was like I was trapped on a treadmill. I felt totally stuck.

At lunch one day, she took me shopping and made me try on a new shirt. I'll admit my clothes were old and tired. While I was in the dressing room changing, she took my shirt and threw it away. I was so terrified I couldn't move. She insisted I come with her or we'd be late getting back to school. But I couldn't go out without my special blue shirt. She ended up fishing it out of the garbage can, saying, "You need help."

I couldn't concentrate anymore

A few things did help

Carrie practically dragged me to the school guidance counselor. He referred me to a psychologist who offered a kind of therapy that helps people with compulsions. For the first time in my life, I talked about all the things I was dealing with and how unhappy I was. I was expecting to hear that I had an obsessive-compulsive disorder, just like Carrie, and that's exactly what the psychologist said. It's a type of anxiety disorder. The diagnosis explained my constant need for reassurance, my obsessions, and my inability to throw things out. The psychologist also said that it's rare for people with this condition to be able to fix it on their own.

My life did eventually change

That started me on the way to coping, but the road was full of unexpected turns. I became obsessed with checking my horoscope, convinced that I had a different and better destiny. I worried about germs on my blouse and on the hem of my jeans. I washed my hands fifty times a day.

In a way I was right about my destiny: my life did eventually change, but it took time. The treatment my psychologist gave me was called cognitive behavioral therapy. She taught me techniques for keeping the OCD at bay, ways to answer my obsessive thoughts in my mind without acting them out. It sounds very simple, like, *Think positive thoughts*, but it involves retraining your brain. I needed to do homework—worksheets and exercises—as if I were learning a new language.

More relief came when Carrie started introducing me to other friends with OCD. They're part of my support network now, and a bunch of us are even taking an improv comedy class together.

It helped just to talk about OCD with other people who "got" it. I hoped that telling my parents would also bring relief.

But when I finally found the courage to say, "Mom, I have a compulsive disorder," her face went blank. She sat there frozen, and then suddenly jumped up and moved away. "There's nothing wrong with you," she said. Even today, my parents refuse to acknowledge my diagnosis.

My brother and I are much closer now. We get out of the house and have fun together, hanging out in cafés or taking the bus downtown. We've decided that even though we can't talk about our feelings as a family, the two of us can be there for each other.

I'm finally getting unstuck. Life is definitely getting better.

Applause

BEN

I was a child star. Man, did I love the spotlight. I craved the attention, was addicted to it. I needed everyone to know that I was the brightest, the most talented kid around. In high school, I continued to do it all—write music, star in plays, make record demos. Cool, right? I was a time bomb ready to explode.

I grew up in Niagara Falls, Ontario—not exactly Hollywood North. Nobody in my family was even remotely connected to show business so my parents and my older brother must have been puzzled when I asked for an agent. I was only five and I didn't shut up about it until they found somebody to represent me. By the time I was six, they were driving me to Toronto for auditions.

It turned out to be more than a whim: I worked as an actor for a lot of my childhood. My cherubic face and eagerness to please nabbed me roles on TV series and in professional theater. It was an unusual life and, for a long time, a little twisted. I felt sorry for every kid who wasn't me. I really did see myself as the star of the playground. Everyone else was a secondary character.

Hogging the spotlight

In elementary school I got my first clue that I was living in a make-believe world. For the first time in my life I had to share the limelight in a classroom jam-packed with attention seekers. They all seemed to think they deserved the spotlight, too. All of a sudden I wasn't so confident. I reassured myself, *I'm the greatest! No one else has anything on me!* But inside, I started to worry.

That's when I started playing music, writing songs, and teaching myself guitar. It was all about showing the other kids that I was special. My dad created a little recording studio for me in the basement. I'd make an album on the weekend, all in one take. I'd bring it to school and boast to the class, "Ten tracks by Ben. I'm going to have a number-one album in Europe in a year. You'll see." Even at seven and eight, it was exhausting keeping up the façade that only *I* belonged in the spotlight. But I was deathly afraid of what would happen to me if that light went out. *What if I'm a nobody? What if no one notices me?*

At the end of fourth grade I was cast in a TV movie. Ego boosted, I was back to being Golden Boy. When anyone had a problem with me, I decided they were jealous. Without even realizing it, I ditched my best friends.

I was spoiled and I loved every minute of it. After every audition my parents gave me a toy. I loved going out for dinner, because strangers would often recognize me. I smiled and waited for the inevitable "You're so cute!"

Adolescence hits hard

Then I turned thirteen. Suddenly, I wasn't so cute anymore. As my voice changed and my adorable boyishness slipped away, I felt my confidence dissolve. My music, and everything else in my life, felt stale and stupid. I became self-righteous and judgmental, lashing out at other people. I'd hone in on another kid's size, or the way he walked or talked. Any weakness was fair game for me to mock—anything, really, that took the focus off my own insecurities.

Nobody took me aside and said, *What's going on? Let's get to the root of it.* Nobody said, *Chill, it's going to be okay.* Instead I got warning shots from my teachers: "If you keep it up, this is what's going to happen to you …" I felt horrible about some of the stuff I said and did, but I couldn't stop it. I was transforming from Golden Boy to Bully Boy, but the only way I knew to stay on top was by tearing everybody else down. In the end, bullying my classmates only made my anxiety worse. As it became clear that many of them hated me, I started hating myself.

> I felt like a robot

Overload

The summer before high school I promised myself I'd stop being mean. The problem was, when I suppressed those angry urges, I didn't feel anything. *All* my emotions seemed to disappear. I felt like a robot.

Alone in my basement studio, I kept making music. Night after night, I would turn off all the lights and listen to myself sing. My parents were insanely supportive, sometimes to a fault. They didn't seem to mind that the songs I wrote became weirder and weirder. It was kind of crazy. I remember thinking, *I wish my dad would notice that I'm suffering.* He could have recognized the symptoms if he'd been looking at me the right way, but he wore rose-colored glasses. I guess he liked thinking of me as a creative genius as much as I did. I held that against him for a few years.

Hardly anybody ever asked me to hang out anymore. Every day my brother and I would watch TV together in silence and then go back to our own thing. I had no idea that he was having a rough time in high school, too. We didn't talk to each other when we most needed it.

I convinced myself I was making an amazing record demo that would show everyone how great I really was. What I was actually doing was shutting out my anxiety, that fear always in the back of my mind that maybe I *wasn't* the greatest thing on earth. I thought if my demo was a success, I could handle anything.

I was so wrapped up in impressing others that I didn't even notice when Freddie, the guinea pig I'd had for years, died. I was getting ready for Battle of the Bands, a music competition at school, when I realized that Freddie's cage was gone from the rec room. Freddie had been a constant presence in my life. I had made up cartoon shows about him and doodled guinea pigs everywhere. I had even made a guinea-pig card game that I sold to my classmates for two bucks a pack. When I asked my mom where he was, she told me that he'd died two weeks ago. How could I not have noticed? I thought, *Things I love die because I'm such an asshole.*

On top of all this, the roles that had come my way so easily became scarce. I didn't have that to fall back on anymore, or anything else. I had pushed away my old friends. No wonder they didn't like me. *I* didn't like me.

By this point everything made me anxious. In class I couldn't keep still. My lips trembled and I got the shakes. I felt like I was

always on stage, flubbing my lines and my timing. I even had to force myself to do what I used to love most—music. I got lost in a vicious cycle of trying to get back "the old self" I thought was so much better. But he was gone. All of a sudden, everyone around me seemed so much fucking cooler. Even when someone did show interest in me, I screwed it up. When this girl I liked asked me out, I broke our date with a lame excuse. I'd gone from thinking that nobody was good enough to be with me to being convinced that it was me who wasn't good enough to be with anyone else.

Sleepwalking through life

In the middle of my sophomore year in high school, I landed a role in a comedy revue at a big theater. But my heart wasn't in it. Now I really *was* acting—pretending to be my younger self. Another performer, a funny, sweet man whom I idolized, took me aside and said, "I know growing up is hard." He was reaching out to me but I wouldn't open up to him. I was like, "What are you talking about? Everything is fine!"

During the run, I lived in cast housing downtown. I'd wake up, do the show, then go home to my little apartment and watch *Star Trek* or something. Over and over again, the same thing, like I was on autopilot. I felt like I was sleepwalking through my life and I couldn't bring myself to care. Even the applause couldn't make up for the hollow I'd dug myself into.

In my junior and senior years I made the Top 40 on *Canadian Idol*. That helped a little, but without any friends to celebrate with, I found it didn't matter much. I lost all my self-respect. I was just a performing puppet. Without real interaction with anybody else, my anxiety and depression just kept growing. I'd spend every minute I could lying in my room, lights off, listening to my own voice coming over the sound system. I kept thinking, *I can deal with it. This year will be different.* But I didn't understand that feeling connected to other human beings was what I needed most.

Just letting go

From the time I could talk, I had been a big fish in a small pond. In high school I was a medium-sized fish. When I got to college

> "No expectations, just have fun"

I felt like a minnow. The campus was huge and alienating, more intimidating than I was willing to admit. Nobody cared about the commercials I'd done or the movies or TV shows.

For years I'd been terrified that I'd become a nobody. Then in college a strange thing happened. I stopped caring about that. I was just another student, and that turned out to be okay. More than okay. By the end of my first year, when I finally found a good friend, I realized that I had something to offer besides my voice and my ability to act.

For a long time I had hung on to the idea that artists were a different species, and that I was one of the chosen ones. I thought that to be great I had to suffer. I was obsessed with perfection and control, with having my life proceed just one way. Suddenly, it just occurred to me that it didn't have to be so. Maybe it takes more courage to decide *not* to suffer. One time when I was finishing a music project, I was feeling dissatisfied with everything I was turning out. My friend said, "No expectations, just have fun." I tried that and it worked a lot better.

It really impressed me how much a simple shift in perspective had helped. I decided to learn more about how the mind works. I found out that, like many people, I'd been letting negative thought patterns guide my actions for years.

I met a guy who complained bitterly about his mom. Even when she put dinner down in front of him, he was convinced she was trying to control him. I thought, *This guy's deluded. It's obviously not true. His assumptions are way off.*

Then I realized that I had a similar thing going with *my* father. I'd always resented my dad. Even before he opened his mouth, I'd dismissed what he had to say. I took a hard look at where that idea came from, and remembered a time when I was four years old. I wanted to drive his car and he wouldn't let me. My four-year-old brain took that as a sign he didn't trust me. From then on, I set out to prove to the world that I should be the exception to the rule. I would be special. Even my motivation for choosing the arts wasn't as authentic as I'd thought! I spent the next fifteen years completely self-absorbed.

That insight empowered me to call my dad and apologize. I took him out for coffee and actually listened to him for the first time, and felt all the love he had for me and I had for him.

A lot of good things have happened since then. I've learned to stop and explore what's going on inside me, to find the quiet amid all the noise and chatter inside my head. I've learned that my anxious or depressed feelings don't have to control me. I can find peace and self-acceptance no matter what my situation is.

We let our insecurities rob us of that power at times, but we can get it back again. It's about finding a new perspective and changing the way you think. I've started a monthly improv night that encourages people, flaws and all, to fully embrace the human condition. Most of the people who perform have struggled with emotional issues, just as I have.

It was hard let go of the beautiful shining boy who got all the applause. But I guess you could say I've figured out how to join the human race. I have great friends who really care about me. My life feels meaningful. I don't know if I'll make performing my career, but if I do, I will never let the applause define who I am.

(Dis)Comfort Zone

NEEMA

I was a stranger in my own life, living in a home where I didn't feel safe, inside a body I didn't understand. For a long time, there wasn't any place I felt okay. It was a formula for crippling anxiety.

I'm from Texas, the only child of a black mother and a white father. Growing up in Austin, I was closer to my mom's world, a pretty tight community of East Africans—mostly Kenyans—with lots of aunties and uncles. Every month or so there would be a big potluck in one of their backyards. Everyone would crowd together at picnic tables over slabs of roast goat and *irio*, fried pieces of mashed corn, potatoes, and greens. I knew that they loved me, and I adored them. But deep down, I felt different. It wasn't that their accents and memories didn't match up with my own Texas upbringing. It was as if I belonged in some other culture I hadn't found yet. Still, I loved the bawdy stories and teasing chatter of those long afternoons.

Expectations

The smiles died away when we got back home. Our house wasn't much of a place for laughing. My dad was kind of a loner. When he came home from work, he'd spend hours by himself playing the guitar. He was also unpredictable. I never really knew why. All I knew was that a forgotten glass of juice, too-loud music, or a bike left on the lawn would light his fuse. He would yell and throw things and break things. I tried hard not to set him off. I didn't dare talk back to him or argue with him. There was no telling what would happen if I did.

I did fight with my mom. At least she didn't scare me! But Mom was a force in her own right. She had strict notions of who she wanted me to be: obedient, modest, and an excellent student.

Like an insect with twitching antennae, I was constantly on the alert, trying to sense the vibes between my mom and my dad, and their reactions to me. I tried to be as perfect as possible. When I didn't meet their expectations, which was often, I got anxious—feelings of panic, tightness in my chest, the sweats. This was accompanied by such deep self-loathing that I would lose my voice. I considered running away. I was depressed and thought of suicide.

Gender matters

Middle school can be hard for anyone, but for a person with anxiety and depression, it can be hell. I didn't yet know the words for what I was suffering, but I was struggling with both. I thought my misery was normal, what everyone went through. Plus I was so bored in class that my grades were in the tank. My parents were so preoccupied with my grades and whether my behavior was acceptable that they never gave much thought to what was causing my unhappiness.

My middle school had kids of every shade, so my café-au-lait color was not a big deal. That didn't mean I wasn't bullied. It began when everybody's bodies started to change. The other kids must have sensed that I felt uncomfortable in my own skin, a female body that seemed to belong to somebody else. It was as if they realized it before I did. Suddenly gender mattered. It took me by surprise. What did it mean to be *a girl*? I didn't know.

Trying to act tough

My reaction to the bullying was to become really tough. I started hanging out with kids with street smarts. The Mexican girls, the *chicanas*, projected a very specific don't-mess-with-me attitude. It was sexy and strong and hard and I wanted to copy it.

These girls made the bullies back off, but my parents were worried. They and my aunties and uncles went on a campaign to make me more feminine: softer and more demure. They bought me "appropriate" clothes that remained unworn in my drawer. If I wore a skirt (because my other stuff was dirty), they just about did cartwheels.

Without quite knowing whom I should please, I spent a lot of time figuring out how to be the best girl I could be, desperately studying magazine articles with titles like "Your Perfect Skin Routine" and "Six Weeks to Amazing Thighs." I mimicked the way the girls walked on TV. I copied the kids in my class, trying to fling my hair the way the prettiest girl did until she threatened to tell the principal I was making fun of her.

None of it worked. I came off looking foolish and feeling miserable. That cycle of judgment and self-loathing started churning again.

Finding a niche (sort of)

I arrived at high school dejected and confused. But in some ways the big sprawling campus was an improvement. I had teachers who gave me actual work. At least I had the distraction of serious assignments. It kept my mind off my worries.

By now I had figured some things out about being a girl. It meant wearing makeup and tight clothes and trying to be desirable. I knew I was supposed to like guys and have crushes on them. I stuck pictures of pop stars in my room. In freshman year, I was invited on a real date by a decent-looking guy named Trev. The thought of being alone with him terrified me: *Would he like how I looked? Would I say something stupid?* In a shaky frenzy I got dressed, put on eye makeup, and brushed out my hair. It was weird going through the motions for a guy I felt no real attraction to. The date was a disaster; I could barely speak. The highlight was going back to my house and watching a fishing show. I couldn't wait for Trev to go.

I appeared to have the girly-girl act down. But inside, I was always anticipating the worst. My antennae were still working overtime. If I felt any twinge of disapproval, I'd clam up or make for the exit. Inside the classroom I often felt like a trapped animal. Sometimes panic would rise up: I'd feel nauseous and overwhelmed by the need to escape.

I could be truthful

I had one friend who always made me feel safe. I met Paula through choir. She was a little older and I leaned on her a lot. On days I felt panicky, I sought her company. She never judged and that helped me calm down. Paula wasn't like the other kids I knew at school. She didn't buy into mainstream attitudes about gender and sexuality. And I could tell she didn't buy my girly act. She encouraged me to ask questions and explore.

That year I started writing stories online. It was scary at first, but you could say it's where I discovered my tribe. Everyone needs to feel safe and part of something. I joined a community of writers, where my online character interacted with characters created by other members. I found out that I liked writing collaboratively. I noticed I wasn't the only one obsessed with what other people thought. The nice thing about being online was that I didn't have to put on makeup or my skinny jeans. Since it was anonymous, I felt I could be truthful. I trusted that the other members, in turn, were being relatively honest. Generally, it's hard to make up the sucky parts.

I discovered love

It was a relief not having to deal with "real" people. I never felt as anxious writing on the web as I did during face-to-face encounters at school. I kept studying what the other girls did, hoping I'd get the hang of being popular. By sophomore year I had flirted with a few boys. I knew more or less what the moves were—even if I didn't feel anything.

I had never in my life met anyone who was gay, so it was a surprise when, over smoothies at the mall, my friend Paula told me she was a lesbian. I didn't know what to say so I didn't say much of anything. But as the weeks went by, I shocked myself when I kept wanting to flirt with her. I didn't know what it meant. When another friend confided to me that she also liked Paula, I was like, *No! That's not fair! I want this.*

I had to make a decision. Was I serious? Was I going to run away from confrontation (like I always did) or do something about my feelings? Knowing someone else liked Paula sort of put a time crunch on things and that's how I came out: I told Paula I thought I might be gay and she asked me how I knew. Very awkwardly, I said it was because I had a big crush on her. She said she liked me, too. We became a couple. It was amazing to finally be in love.

I worried it would *not be okay*

Paula gave me space to figure out who I was. I still felt very anxious about people's judgments of me, but I could talk to her about it. She reassured me that I was lovable, that my fears weren't founded in reality. "I think you're great," she told me. "You don't have to worry about what others think of you." She was a good person who really cared about me. From then on I felt the anxiety that gripped me start to ebb. The panic attacks came less often and I made some new friends.

As time passed, I noticed there was a split between the kids in my class who were actually okay with my being gay, and the ones who pretended to be okay but were actually freaked out by it. I worried it would *not be okay* at home, so I kept my new identity a secret from my parents. I wasn't sure how they'd react and didn't want to find out.

Coming out

Mom's culture was not accepting of homosexuality, so I was in no rush to bring it up. Seeing her disappointed yet again would just give me another thing to be anxious about. It came about almost by accident, in the car on the way home one day. I had been out to lunch with my mom, telling her how some of my friends were questioning their sexuality. I guess I was being less subtle than I thought. "Are you wondering about your own sexuality?" she asked. Because she asked me so directly, I could not lie. Her calm reaction was the last thing I expected. Still, I could sense concern. Later, I overheard her talking to other parents about it. She worried that I would face discrimination. She hoped it was a phase.

The bigger surprise was my dad. I'd gotten better at avoiding his dark moods, but for years we'd spent hardly any time together. Late one Saturday night I sat down beside him on the couch. He was playing his guitar, and when he stopped to tune a string, I blurted out, "I'm gay." All he did was nod. Given the problems we'd had, that was a huge relief. When I got up to go to bed, he took my hand and held it for a minute.

Once I was out to my parents, I didn't have any more secrets. Paula being in my life gave me self-confidence; I wasn't charting other people's reactions all the time. For a while, high school was pretty smooth sailing.

Learning to cope

I thought I would never feel anxious again. But it came rushing back when I was a senior. I was devastated. I had to apply to college, and the stress triggered the old panic. I'd feel light-headed and nauseous, or sometimes my arms and legs went numb. I had this overwhelming fear, like the world was about to end. One day I forgot my locker combination and burst into tears in the hallway. I almost missed my English essay deadline and frantically pulled an all-nighter to get it done. When I messed up like that, I was ashamed and depressed. At times I didn't think I could stand the pain.

Somehow, I managed to keep going. Staying focused on the task in front of me kept the anxiety from overtaking me. Feeling supported by Paula and my parents helped, too. So did getting into a college that I liked. But what really made a difference was finding a good therapist. My mother asked our doctor to recommend someone. Being a mixed-race gay woman isn't the easiest way to go through life, but that wasn't the only reason for my panic attacks. It turned out that I have an anxiety disorder.

My panic attacks won't last forever

I'm in my early twenties now. I've learned to manage my panic, my intense desire to run away. Some things are always going to make me anxious, like being around people I don't know well, or in situations where I'll be judged. The best thing is just to let it happen. Even at the worst times, when I'm most anxious, I know that it's going to end. My panic attacks won't last forever. The more I obsess about them and try to find the answer that will "fix" me, the less happy I am.

To control my anxiety now, I go to therapy and I practice meditation and breathing. I know that I can't just depend on other people to manage my panicky feelings. Meditation allows my obsessive thoughts to pass by. Instead of picking them up and worrying about them, I'll say to myself, *Oh, this is making me feel really anxious*. Then I'll try to let my mind move on to the next thing.

It takes time to figure this stuff out. It's impossible to escape all the stress life throws at you, but I'm walking proof that you can learn to deal with it and find a place of refuge within yourself.

Changing Course

OLLIE

I'm not a naturally stressed-out person, but high school can make a wreck out of anyone. I was always finding myself in stressful situations. I survived by devising a game plan and sticking to it. It was when I got to college that things fell apart.

At fourteen, I was clueless about how to organize my time, and as the pace of high school sped up, I dug myself into a deeper hole. I'd freak out when I discovered an important assignment was due the next day. Some weeks I had so much work I didn't even know where to begin. I'd go for days without seeing any friends, which only added to my stress. Sometimes the pressure was too much and I'd break down and cry. My dad often came to my rescue. Once, late at night, he held a flashlight in the backyard while I recorded the nocturnal migration of earthworms.

But I learned. Occasional catastrophic failure—having to make up a speech on the spot about the causes of World War I, for instance—can be a great teacher. As I went from year to year, I figured out how to minimize the freak-outs, reduce the tears, lessen the anxiety. The secret was stress management. I boiled it down to a few basic rules.

Rule #1 was keeping my life in perspective. Any day that I had two free periods, I'd use one of them for work and the other for not-work. During the second period I'd leave school, hop on a trolley, and walk around a part of town I'd never been in before. A big part of stress management is figuring out what your triggers are. Being in school reminded me constantly of the work I had to do. Getting out of those four walls just for an hour in the middle of the day, and getting some exercise, was a big help. I also made time every day to talk to my friends, no matter how much work I had to do.

Rule #2 was knowing myself. I noticed that when I was bored or under-committed, I got less done. Taking on more, rather than less, forced me to be efficient. I ran for student council and threw myself into

I'd made a big mistake

extracurricular programs. It was a relief to have things on my plate that weren't homework. It also meant I had to budget my time more carefully and—surprise!—I did better on my assignments.

Rule #3 was checking my breaking point—knowing when I was about to lose it and calming myself down before I did. When a huge project was due, I'd typically get so stressed I couldn't even start on it. To take my mental temperature, I asked myself, "Am I too wired right now to be efficient?" If the answer was yes (which it often was), I'd say, "Okay, I'm going to go pick up a juice and take a walk." I'd leave whatever was causing me stress, calm down, and then come back to it. I didn't say, "I can't take a break! I have twenty pages left!" Punishing myself was a no-win.

Using this system I didn't merely survive high school, I aced it. But none of these rules applied when I got to college and discovered I'd made a big mistake.

Knocked off my game

I wanted to study journalism. I picked a school with one of the best programs in the country and applied. I couldn't believe that I got in.

My parents and I crammed a rent-a-truck with my stuff and drove to the city that would be my new home. My posters went up on the dorm-room walls. I got myself a tiny fridge and stocked up on noodles. Yeah, I was ready, except for one thing: my heart wasn't in it. I hated the city. I hated the big, impersonal campus with its brutal concrete buildings and the windy, boring walks between them. The other kids were okay, but it was the wrong kind of place for me, the wrong style of teaching. I put up with classes taught by graduate students who had no experience as working journalists. I told myself, "I guess this is what college life is supposed to be like."

Crisis

Then, as I was preparing for a second year of misery, I woke up. Or rather, I didn't.

At the beginning of August I quit my summer job installing sprinkler systems so that I'd have a break before school started. The first morning I stayed in bed, reveling in the unscheduled hours stretching ahead of me. The second morning, I felt a bit guilty, but slept in anyway. As the week passed, I still couldn't get out of bed. Except for trips to the fridge and the bathroom, I was a slug.

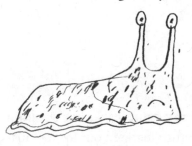

I had absolutely no energy. I couldn't get excited about seeing anybody or doing anything. I'd think about riding my bike or going for a swim, and then I'd roll over and go back to sleep. My parents were concerned, but I convinced them that I was taking a much-needed break.

Guilt and anxiety welled up in me when Mom and Dad drove three hours on their own to find me an apartment. They spent the hottest day of the year traipsing through the neighborhood around the campus while I lay in my dark bedroom listening to Coldplay. They signed a lease, bought a couch, chairs, and a bed, and stocked my new kitchen with tubs of frozen spaghetti sauce and chili, all while I couldn't find the energy to get out of bed.

I had no further plans

The sick feeling inside me wouldn't let up. That's when I had my revelation: I didn't want to go back to school.

I changed out of my pajamas and went to the patio to tell my parents. The timing couldn't have been more awkward, but I knew there was never going to be a good moment to say, "Mom and Dad, guess what? I want to break the lease on the apartment I haven't even seen yet. I don't want to go back to the prestigious college I was lucky to get into."

My parents were speechless. They hadn't seen this coming. Nor had I. And the stark reality was that I had no further plans. It was the most massively stressful thing I'd ever done in my life. I had been counting on this career path for at least two years. I'd thought I had my whole future planned out and suddenly I had nothing.

Decision time

Once I made the decision, my energy came back, but so did a feeling of panic. I *liked* having my future mapped out for me, just as I'd liked organizing my time. Now I was peering into a void and freaking out because I didn't know what to do with the rest of my life.

> I *liked* having my future mapped out

I saw an ad for teaching English in Indonesia. My parents were not enthusiastic so I scrapped that idea and proposed moving to Australia. Too far, too expensive. I looked into being a crew member of a cargo ship. No qualifications.

"Never mind," I said. "I'm moving to London." I'd been there once before. I booked a flight. My parents weren't thrilled, but at least we had relatives there who could put me up until I got on my feet. A college dropout with absolutely no experience at anything except lawn sprinklers (useless to a country where it rains daily), I boarded a plane, meager savings in hand, for one of the world's most expensive cities.

My cousin James grudgingly let me stay on his sticky kitchen floor. "Just one week if you don't mind," he said. I left his tiny flat at 8:00 every morning and spent all day on my feet handing résumés to managers. I got home at about 8:00 p.m. and stayed up until midnight applying for jobs online. I'd arrived in London sure I would find a job in a city that big. Wrong! Two weeks and three hundred applications later, I hadn't received a single offer.

The final straw

James was getting fed up. The final straw came when I used my debit card at a restaurant and it was declined. He had to bail me out. My parents hadn't wanted me to leave college in the first place, so they weren't about to underwrite my dubious adventures. If I didn't find a way to make money, I would have to give up living in London and go home. I dreaded the thought of moving back in with my mom and dad, tail between my legs. I had to keep this impending sense of doom from over-whelming me.

I made a last-ditch attempt to find work. I broadened my search, applying for jobs anywhere in the UK. Within twenty-four hours I got an e-mail from a Mrs. Brody. She ran a five-bedroom, three-hundred-year-old inn in central Scotland, in a town of twelve people. The job on offer was hotel assistant. I would be one of only two staff—in effect, the waiter, bartender, receptionist, concierge, cook, and pastry chef. I had zero ex-perience at any of these, but if she was willing to take a chance on me, so was I.

I had no way to reach anybody

Working it out

"When can you start?" said Mrs. Brody over the phone.

"My bags are packed already," I said. "I'll be on the next train." I bought a ticket with my last twenty pounds.

I'd never been to Scotland. I was the only passenger to get off at my stop, in the middle of a field. No station, just a concrete slab. I couldn't see anything for miles: no houses, no phone booth. Just fields. There was a road that ran parallel to the tracks but there was no sign of civilization in any direction.

I slumped down on the bags that held all my worldly possessions. It started to rain. Foolishly, I'd been listening to music on my phone during the whole train ride so it had very little battery life. I couldn't even check my e-mail for Mrs. Brody's phone number. I had no way to reach anybody and no way of knowing what direction to walk in. I couldn't even get on the next train: it only came once every two days. And I was getting drenched.

I could feel panic rising in my throat. *I'm going to fall asleep in the rain and drown*, I thought. *Are there wild animals in Scotland? I will die here. What have I done to myself?*

A half hour later a jeep shuddered to a stop in front of me. By that point I was crying. With a cheerful "Oh, sorry I'm late. Did the train come on time? It never does," Mrs. Brody tossed my bags into the back and motioned to me to get in. She took me to the hotel and showed me my room, a converted walk-in closet. It had a sawed-off bed because a full bed wouldn't fit.

I was completely wiped. I woke up the next morning and discovered that the closet contained another sawed-off bed. I had slept next to a 300-pound Polish man with facial piercings and tattoos—my roommate. I had not been introduced, let alone warned about him. At first I thought, *I'm at home now and I'm not going to die.* Then I thought, *I might!* The man woke with a snort and raised a pierced eyebrow at me. I soon found out he was a totally nice guy. His name was Jozef and we got along splendidly.

I stayed at Mrs. Brody's for five months, working six days a week. When she closed up to move to Majorca, I didn't panic; I found other jobs around England and Scotland. It was a hilarious and ridiculous time. I did clerical work in an employment agency, ran a library reading program for little kids, packed chocolates, and baled hay. I learned a lot about the work and people and environments I liked best—towns rather than cities, and employers that valued independent thinking. This led me to find a college program that was a much better fit.

During those months of rambling, I banished the anxiety that had once pinned me to my bed. Once I realized that there's no one right way to live your life, I found some peace of mind. My year of adventure taught me that I have enough skills to put a roof over my head and to feed myself. I did what my heart told me to do, I took risks, and I worked harder than I ever thought I could. Now I know that I'm resilient enough to deal with the stress that life throws at me—even the stress I create for myself.

Nowhere to Hide

CAROLINE

My older brother left home when I was ten. I didn't miss him. He had never paid much attention to me, and I loved having my parents all to myself. It suited them, too. Like me, my mom was painfully shy, so she and my father hardly ever socialized. And I would much rather watch a movie at home with my mom and dad than be with friends my own age. I could relax and joke around—which I found almost impossible to do when I left the house. My family sheltered me from the sea of people outside our door.

Anxiety took center stage in my life in sixth grade, when I was the first girl in my class to need a bra. As a shy kid who hated to stand out, this really threw me. Yes, I had been told about the physical changes of puberty, but nobody had ever talked about the emotional fallout of being so different. Not my mom, not my teachers. I felt betrayed by that silence. The unfairness of it made me want to scream, but my rage got stuck in my throat. Every morning I woke up feeling anxious and it stayed that way all day. When anxiety is part of your daily existence, it starts to feel normal.

Moving to a combined middle and high school held out the promise of relief. I thought I'd blend in better where there were older girls. But when it was time for back-to-school shopping, I got even more self-conscious. I'd never worn skirts or anything girly and that was the standard uniform at the new school. In the store with my mother, trying on the uniform, my heart started to race and blood rushed to my head. I started to cry, confused and threatened by this new person I was being asked to be. I realize now, in retrospect, that I was having my first anxiety attack. They became a semiregular thing.

I refused to wear the skirt and insisted that my mother buy me the pants option instead. But when I got to school, none of the other girls were wearing the pants.

I desperately wanted to blend in

The only thing worse than wearing the skirt was calling attention to myself, so I bought the skirt after all. But it wasn't enough. I wanted to be like everyone else, especially the cool kids, with their in-jokes. They smoked at lunchtime, so I took up smoking, too, hoping to impress. I hated it, and it got me nowhere. Looking back, they must have thought, *Who is this wannabe?*

Two of the cool girls became sort-of friends of mine. "Sort of" because I never knew where I stood. I was constantly worried about saying the wrong thing. If I called one of them, I'd wait by the phone, impatient with worry that she'd never call me back.

When they announced they were getting their ears pierced and invited me to come along, I jumped at the chance. When the day came, I dressed in black because I knew they would, too. I got to the mall early, and immediately felt anxious. I waited for more than an hour, checking the time over and over, sure that everyone was staring at me, wondering why I was all alone. I finally gave up and walked the fifteen blocks home. I learned later that they had gone the day before but hadn't bothered to tell me.

It hurt like hell that they had treated me like dirt, but I kept trying to be friends with them. I didn't feel I had any choice.

Easy target

It's hard to think of a time in middle school when I felt sure of myself for more than a few days. But my confidence took another nosedive in freshman year. One day, a member of the cool crowd came up to me.

"Could you help me?" she asked. "I'm having trouble with this assignment."

We'd never really talked before. I'd figured she didn't like me.

My desire to please made me a pushover, so I helped her with her essay and it snowballed from there. We met in the stairwell behind the gym every Monday morning. I gave her what I'd written for her the night before, and she handed me some new assignment she needed done. I ended up writing all her English essays, in addition to my own. It was a lot of work making them different enough that the teacher wouldn't notice. I figured she would eventually show her appreciation, but it became clear she was just using me.

I wanted to stop doing her homework, but worried what would happen if I did. I fantasized about worst-case scenarios. I knew she was a bully and could manipulate opinion at school. I spent one weekend in a state of high anxiety, absolutely dreading what I had to do. But that Monday, I screwed up my courage and told her I wouldn't help her anymore. Then everything I'd feared might happen did happen. She spread rumors about me: that I was a lesbian and, when my English teacher's laptop went missing, that I had stolen it.

Always anxious

I broke down in tears and told my mom everything. She wanted to go straight to the principal but that made me even more anxious. I begged her not to: I couldn't be a tattletale. That would have been social suicide. Then the girl bragged to somebody about how she had stolen the laptop herself, but set me up. The principal got wind of it and the girl was kicked out of school.

I couldn't be a tattletale

My reprieve didn't last long. Other people had heard her make accusations about me. Maybe they knew I wasn't a thief, but they wondered about my sexual orientation. I started to question how I looked, how I carried myself. *Do I look gay? Do I look straight?*

My anxiety got worse; it hung over me from the moment I left for school until the moment I got home. That feeling you get when you're about to give a speech in front of a bunch of people—the rapid heartbeat, the butterflies, the knot in your stomach, the clammy hands? I was always about to give a speech. It was killing me inside.

Anxiety had already led me to make bad decisions and to question who I was. It was creeping into every part of my life.

Always exposed

I had no close friends. I was so preoccupied I couldn't pay attention to TV, and music sounded like noise. Being out in the world was unbearable; I hardly ever left the path I trudged between home and school. Getting decent grades had always been a given for me, but I even lost confidence in my brain. I was a good writer, but I started feeling no sentence I wrote was natural enough, and writing became a terrible chore. I worried that I wasn't smart enough and didn't know enough.

My brother came home from college for a weekend and asked if I wanted to go for a run with him. I had been running since fourth grade and mostly liked it. But we'd barely gone a block when he said, "Is something wrong? You look different."

I pretended I didn't know what he meant.

"You're hunched over. You keep staring at your feet," he said. "Come on. Are you sure you're okay?"

He was right: I had started to shrink. I held my head down and shuffled. I avoided eye contact. The idea of being *seen*—even just walking across the street—had become excruciating. I believed that people were constantly judging me and I wasn't measuring up. I was so down on myself that I couldn't believe anybody would want to be friends with me. More than anything I wanted to hide.

"Just get over it"

I was having more frequent panic attacks. Blood rushed to my head, I couldn't breathe normally, and I cried a lot. My heart ached, like someone was squeezing it hard. Sometimes an incident would set off an attack, or a lot of little things would stack up and send me over the edge. I now understand how these attacks might have been avoided: I needed someone to listen, to help me get the feelings out. Instead, I tried to keep it all under wraps. No one really knew the extent of my anxiety and shame. Not my brother, not my classmates, not my teachers. Not even my parents.

Even though I was close to my mother and father, it made me feel worse to admit to them that I couldn't cope. One night my dad was helping me with my physics homework. I wasn't getting the concepts and it made me cry. He could see how anxious I was, but he had no idea how much I was worrying. He told me, "We don't care. We love you anyway." But my anxiety always seemed like a weakness. His reassurance didn't really help me at the time.

I must have learned my feelings of shame from my mom. She had experienced anxiety herself growing up and had never had anyone to talk to about it. One Sunday when I was a junior, my mother and I were in the kitchen. I was thinking about the week coming up and suddenly I panicked: a surge of negative thoughts accumulated into a wave that crashed down on me. I started to cry. Mom wasn't particularly sympathetic.

"Stop it. What's bothering you?" she asked.

"I don't know, I just feel terrible."

"No," she said. "It has to be something. Tell me what it is."

"There's no 'it'—it's a lot of things, I guess. My whole life."

She got so frustrated with this answer that she started screaming. Instead of trying to talk to me and calm me down, *she* got anxious. Her only real advice was to dry my eyes, buck up, and get over it. Believe me, if I knew how, I would have done it. I would have given anything not to feel so anxious all the time.

Giving up

My only after-school activity was running track. I wasn't a speed demon, but I had a long stride and good endurance and a decent time in the 400 meter. At the school district's first meet of the year, I paced myself and made a strong push at the end. Much to my surprise, I won the race, finishing way ahead of girls who had beaten me at prior meets. I was thrilled. Then one of my teammates made a snide remark: "Don't get too full of yourself. Last year you came in ninth." Like my win was a fluke. The panic came back again. I believed her.

Because of that win, I advanced to a higher level of competition and my coach told me he thought I could place again. The next meet was eight days away, but it felt like eight months. I couldn't stay still for more than a minute. I was too restless to sleep. The same negative thoughts kept running through my head: *Everyone's counting on me to do well. What if I don't? What if my win was a fluke? What if I come in ninth?*

> I was too restless to sleep

On race day, I arrived at school trembling and teary. "That's normal," my coach reassured me. "I used to throw up before every race I ran in." At the track, as I waited endlessly for my event, I began to hyperventilate. I had pains in my chest and couldn't catch my breath. Cold chills ran through my body, and then that turned to puddles of sweat. I felt like I might suffocate and I told my coach that I couldn't run. Another teacher drove me back to school. I was so ashamed, I quit the team.

Something "real" to worry about

I tried again and again to push down the anxious thoughts but they came out anyway, sometimes in awful ways. I started cutting myself with razors or glass, on my stomach and upper arm so nobody would notice. Anxiety was invisible but this was something I could *see*. And it gave me something else to worry about: it took my mind off my anxiety and the things that were causing it.

It all reached a peak in the spring of senior year. I signed up for the school talent show, to write jokes for the MCs. But by mistake I had signed up to *be* an MC. The idea of going onstage in front of everyone filled me with terrible dread, but it was too late to get out of it.

The night before the talent show I cut up my stomach so that it looked like a crazy road map. Show day was a blur. My insides were in knots, I couldn't look at the audience, and I rushed my jokes, but I got through it. Afterward, I overheard people saying that they didn't like the MCs as much this year. I was sure it was because of me. I couldn't wait for high school to end.

Not the only one

I had a lot I needed to say

High school did end, but I knew something else had to change. That summer I signed up for a workshop on anxiety. I told my story to the group and listened to others tell similar stories. Some were even more drastic than mine. Empathizing with their experiences made me less hard on myself.

For the first time, talking about my worries felt safe. The workshop leader suggested I see a psychiatrist. I was glad that my parents were supportive of the idea, but I would have done it anyway. I realized I had a lot I needed to say, and those weekly sessions gave me enormous relief.

I even told the psychiatrist about the cutting, which I'd kept a secret from everyone. She started me on a low-dose antidepressant. I was finally doing something about the constant worry that hung over me. I learned that exercise helped, and that junk food often made me feel worse. What I put into my body really affects my mood. I'm running again now, and eating better. I don't cut myself anymore.

Through those sessions I realized that I made a lot of negative assumptions about what other people thought about me. But I'm not a mind reader; how can I know what other people think? I don't get caught up in that so much now.

I also tend to "catastrophize," especially about my future. I think, *I'm not going to find a good job. I'm not going to have enough money* ... and then it explodes: *Oh my God! Oh my God!* I've learned to counter those thoughts with optimistic ones.

Choosing to worry less

Once I learned to think more positively, I suddenly found I could write again. That fall, I started a college course in creative writing. I discovered I'm really passionate about it, though I'd been pushing those feelings down for years, out of fear. At first I was self-conscious in class—having to read my work aloud and comparing myself to the other students: the same old story.

But writing turned out to be a great way to put myself out there and see what happens. If people like what I write, fine, but if not, I can *choose* not to worry about that. Funny thing: I've found the less I worry about what people think of me, the more they tend to accept me for who I am.

I had to
figure out
ways to make
myself relax
or I'd snap

Nothing but the Best

LEILA

I've always been competitive. My mantra is *Do well, Do well*. It's what I expect of myself and it's undoubtedly part of my DNA. I'm the only child of two of the most competitive people you can imagine. They are both high-powered trial lawyers who trained all their megawatts of energy on me.

The three of us do everything well, from rock climbing to heli-skiing. Board games around our house are a blood sport. We play "murder" Scrabble. Even our Bouvier dogs get into the act: they've both won agility competitions in a regional dog show.

The best, no matter what

Growing up, my parents always helped make sure I did my best. Sometimes they took it to extremes. For instance, in fifth grade, when I was correcting some math homework, my mother piped up: "If you're going to erase it, erase it well. Don't do a half

job." Even erasing! And when I brought home a mediocre report card, there was practically a family summit to analyze what had gone wrong.

All that intensity could be overwhelming at times. I loved when my parents went away and my grandmother came to take care of me. She made me strawberry milk shakes and butterscotch brownies. We spent hours watching Miyazaki movies or reading Tintin books aloud together. We snuggled into our own safe world where nothing "important" was at stake.

I didn't realize just how much my parents' micromanagement had sheltered me until we moved to a new neighborhood. I didn't know a soul. At my new middle school I was choosy and standoffish and didn't make friends easily. I just wanted to be at home, where things were orderly and predictable. It didn't help that I looked like an alien. I wore orthodontic headgear, and had this big metal appliance strapped to my head and connected to my braces.

Self-conscious and incredibly awkward, I decided I needed a drastic change. I'd worn my straight dark hair below my waist for years, but I thought a cool new hairstyle might be just the ticket. First I experimented with peroxide; then I chopped off my hair above my ears. Not a good look. When I crept downstairs to face my mom, she marched me straight to the salon. But the damage was done. I still remember the tears, and my horrible fear that the other kids would make fun of me, which of course they did.

One fiasco followed another. A new online app was all the rage among the kids at school. It was called Honesty Box, designed to allow people to send each other "honest" messages—anonymously. Colossal mistake! The kids wrote mean and spiteful things to each other in a *Lord of the Flies*–type free-for-all. I didn't even use it, but a girl in my class was convinced I'd sent her a nasty message. "It was definitely you!" she hissed. We got into a fight and she convinced a whole bunch of people in my grade to not talk to me. Their silence made things worse; I'd go to school every day holding my breath, hoping things would change.

I still remember the tears

Coming up short

It was a relief to move on to high school, although, in typical fashion, my parents weren't doing things halfway. They had great faith in my potential, and chose a private girls' school known for its academics. It was a rude awakening, like being thrown into the deep end without a noodle. On the first day in French class the other girls could conjugate verbs I'd never heard of. I sat there with a blank stare on my face, and at the end of class, the teacher pulled me aside.

"Did you understand a word today?" she asked.

"Nope," I said.

It was like that in every class. I'd never had to write an essay or take an exam, which everyone else had obviously been doing forever. I thought, *Uh-oh, I'm in trouble.*

Everyone dressed the same, but beneath the blue sweaters and red kilts, the girls were fiercely competitive. The pressure was coming from all directions: from myself, my parents, and now the other students. Girls would boldly demand, "What did you get on the test?" The teachers posted the names of those who got above 80 and above 90. By process of elimination, everyone knew who *wasn't* doing well.

I had a few shortcomings in the grades department: sciences, math, and languages didn't come easily to me. I even got a low mark in Gym! I had just won third in my age group in a triathlon, but there I was sitting on the gym floor taking a health quiz. Did I do well? No!

In the back of my brain was that constant refrain, *Do well, Do well.* I was my parents' only child! Who besides me could make them proud? I worried all the time: *Have I studied enough? Does four hours a day equal an A, or should it be five hours?* When the math teacher put a test on my desk, I'd stare at it and try not to run from the room. If I didn't do well, I took it very personally.

I was a stretched rubber band

"I got a B minus," I sobbed to Annie, a friend. "The teacher hates me."

By junior year, my stress levels were out of control. I knew my marks really mattered if I wanted to get into a good college, and I'd lie awake in bed at three in the morning, my mind flitting between what I knew and what I didn't know. In my hyperalert state, sensitive to every creak and noise, I knew that my wakefulness was systematically unraveling all the studying I'd just done. I was a stretched rubber band. I *had* to figure out ways to make myself relax or I'd snap.

What worked for me

My parents were both into meditation so my dad would say, "Make sure you're breathing." I'd think, *Obviously I'm breathing.* That just didn't work for me. Through trial and error, though, I figured out other ways to calm myself down. My top three soothing rituals were listening to an audiobook, taking a hot shower, and painting my nails. Sometimes I played the piano. If I let myself drift in one of these pleasant distractions, it usually settled my crazed brain.

A harder task was learning to ask for help. I would sooner have entered a quintathlon than "burden" one of my teachers. Even though my parents were paying a freaking fortune in tuition, I hated admitting to a teacher that I didn't understand something. My parents had taught me how to aim high, but not how to ask for help! I felt so stupid and embarrassed that I practically had to drag myself across the classroom. But I forced myself to show up every day after school for extra coaching and it worked. I learned my lesson big-time. My dreaded math course became my strongest subject.

Moving on and letting go

There was one more thing I had to face. Growing up with parents like mine, I had always had structure. I was used to that environment and if I didn't have that support, I fell apart. Even if I was hanging out with friends, I'd ask, "Okay, what are we doing next?" I didn't care whose plan it was, but there had to be a plan.

Part of my competitiveness was a need to know; I couldn't abide pressure or uncertainty. I had been taught to be prepared. I couldn't write an essay in one night. I couldn't cram for an exam. When I tried, my anxiety levels just killed me.

I admit I was a bit of a control freak in high school, always the responsible one, never the slacker. Sometimes it was a double-edged sword. Two of my friends were party girls. More often than I could count, I lost one of them in the wee hours of the morning and felt the anxiety rise in my chest. *Where is she? What happened? We need to go home.*

It got old after a while, particularly because the worrying didn't go both ways. When I stressed out about an assignment or exam, these friends would say, "That's so stupid. Who cares?" Or, "Don't worry. I haven't studied for that." I'd say, "What! You haven't studied yet? This is 40 percent of our mark!" Eventually, I got sick of worrying on their behalf. I got tired of being their mom.

I got sick of worrying

In senior year I won the role of Hippolyta in *A Midsummer Night's Dream*, acting with a group of girls I hadn't known that well. To my surprise, we got along great. I discovered they were responsible and thought for themselves; they didn't gossip or undermine one another. We became close and spent a lot of time together, studying, having sleepovers, and partying in moderation. These friendships, founded on mutual support and respect, were a much better fit.

Doing *my best without always* being *the best*

Now that I'm in college, my perspective has evolved again. Nobody's looking over my shoulder, nobody's making sure I'm doing everything right. I live in a dorm with a few hundred other people. No one even notices if I sleep in or go to class, get straight As or fail every course. It's not unusual for someone to be screaming in the hallway on Sunday night while I'm studying for an exam. That sort of thing used to stress me out because it seemed so unfair, but I've learned not to take it personally. Life *is* unfair.

I can't solve every problem and control every outcome. I am human and I mess up. I've learned that a B minus is not the end of the world. *My* best doesn't have to be *the* best. Maybe I'll try harder next time. Whatever happens, I'll get another chance.

Obsessions

STEVEN

My anxiety could have killed me, but it didn't. I turned to drugs for relief, but I was the last person who should have. My mom is the reason I'm not living on the street today, or dead.

Mom is an anxious person, like me. She's the type who checks the stove and the front door all the time. Her anxiety led her to shelter me as I was growing up. My mom was convinced that she could only keep me safe if she could see me, so I wasn't allowed to play alone in our yard or walk to the corner store or play at another kid's house.

I was a shy kid, easily frightened. I never wanted to try anything new. Once, at a street fair, the other kids were clustered around a policeman on a horse, patting the horse's nose. When my mom asked me if I wanted to pat the horse, too, I said, "No, he might bite me or step on me." I always feared the worst. On the day I started school, I clung to my mom while the teacher tried to peel my fingers from her shoulders. I wailed, "I don't want my mom to leave." My mother cried as hard as I did. This went on for months.

I didn't even know that anxiety had a name until my parents split up when I was eight. I was furious with my dad because I thought the divorce was his fault. I was sent to a psychologist because of the anger. Behind my anger, of course, was my anxiety, but at that age I wasn't ready for therapy. I'd talk about anything other than what was actually bothering me. Or I wouldn't talk at all. All I wanted was to go skateboarding.

Who cares?

The year my parents split up, my mom sent me to a private boys' school outside Boston. It was old and steeped in tradition and I hated every single ivy leaf that covered the place. The other boys made fun of me because I was short and thin and looked young for my age. The teachers were supposed to make "men" of us, which some of them took to mean they could bully us. My gym teacher yelled at me for having the wrong-color gym socks. He made me cry in front of the class. That did it. I was toast.

After that, every morning when the bus pulled up at the school, I felt a sense of doom so heavy it would make me tremble and feel faint. I was terrified that I'd be ridiculed again. For the first time in my life, I was also terrified of failing. I was smart, but homework made me so anxious I just wouldn't do it. Instead I said, "Fuck it. I'm too cool. I just won't do this and then I won't have to feel bad." Other kids would ask me what mark I got. "I didn't hand it in," I'd say. "Who cares?"

The school had lots of rules I wasn't interested in following. In eighth grade I was captivated by music from the sixties and the hippie movement. I started to play the guitar and let my hair grow long. The administration eventually kicked me out. They said I didn't fit the school's image, and they were right.

After I got kicked out of private school, I started living with my dad and going to a big public high school near the ocean. That's when I got into drugs. As an ex-hippie, my dad was okay with me smoking marijuana as long as I limited it to weekends. It didn't seem to be a problem at that point.

My new school was a refreshing change from the preppy hell of the private school. I had a lot more in common with the other students. I was still shy and withdrawn, and being around girls was a challenge—I would stutter and become tongue-tied. But my anxiety wasn't as visible and I came out of my shell a bit. I made friends pretty quickly, including people who liked to use marijuana as much as I did.

That's when I got into drugs

These friends often came home with me at lunchtime to smoke dope since the house was empty while my dad was at the office. My grades had been pretty bad at my old school, but I wasn't smoking during the day then. Now my grades were in the toilet. As time went on I became more and more interested in getting high.

By sophomore year I had stopped paying attention in school. It didn't seem to matter. The school was much less strict and the classes were easier. Teachers were tolerant and even made jokes about my substance use. I never got into trouble for going to class stoned.

I started out using drugs to rebel and to be part of a cool subculture. But drugs very quickly became important to me as a way of relieving my anxiety. I was trying to cope with so many bad feelings that never went away. When I found a substance that gave me a quick fix, I grabbed it for dear life. I went from smoking joints to abusing amphetamines, cocaine, ketamine, MDMA (Ecstasy), hallucinogens, and opiates.

One part anxiety, two parts paranoia

By the end of junior year, cocaine had become my drug of choice. There were high school kids who wanted to buy drugs so the dealers came into the school grounds to find them. That's how I was getting a lot of my stuff. Then I did cocaine all summer long, too, and really got hooked on it.

My drug habit was expensive, but lucky for me, my parents gave me a generous allowance. They thought I was just smoking weed. By the time they found out I was spending my money on cocaine, it was too late for them to stop me.

By now my anxiety was much worse—so severe that I could barely stand it. It was the reason I did cocaine every day. For a half hour after doing a line of cocaine, you feel confident and invincible, which you don't feel when you're anxious. But the comedown from a cocaine high is a paranoid, terrible experience, and my anxiety made it that much worse. I took more cocaine to avoid those terrible feelings, which is part of what makes it so addictive.

The more of the drug I had in my system, the more paranoid thoughts I had. When I rode the train, I was terrified my hair would get caught in the doors and I'd be dragged down the tracks. I thought escalators would swallow my feet. I thought cranes would crash down on me. I took more and more of the drug to make those feelings go away.

When I went back to school in September, I was too stoned to find the right classroom. That was so painfully embarrassing that I didn't want to go back. Instead, I hung out with friends from another school who were also using a lot of drugs. After missing a month of classes I realized I would never catch up. It was too late. Meanwhile, I was developing a tolerance to cocaine and my addiction got worse.

My parents threatened to stop my allowance if I didn't stay in school, so I transferred to a program for troubled kids. It was closer to my house than the other school and hard drugs were even easier to get there because so many other kids were using them, too. My house was once again the place to hang out with friends and use drugs.

From user to abuser

Over that year I "progressed" to using crack cocaine and my paranoia reached a new level. I finally told my parents that I was having panic attacks. They had me tested and my score showed that I had very severe anxiety. I started seeing a psychiatrist who gave me antidepressant medicine. I didn't tell him I was still doing cocaine. I was playing with my brain but I didn't care about the serious risks involved in combining the two drugs.

I stayed at the alternative program for two years, doing outrageous stuff, skipping class to get high or to buy drugs. I even used the bathroom to freebase cocaine. When the school administrators found out, they'd had enough.

I was having panic attacks

The principal called me down to his office. My parents were there. At this point they knew what was going on. The principal advised my parents to let me become homeless. He believed that was the only way I'd ever learn my lesson. My dad was kind of like, "Okay. Maybe that's a good idea." My mom was like, "Fuck that! No way!" Those words might just have saved my life.

A first, faltering step toward getting better

I moved back in with my mom. This was the beginning of the absolutely vital support she gave me, but it took a while to pay off. Our first step was to move to a new neighborhood, away from my old drug haunts. But that didn't work for long. Different dealers knew I was buying drugs and they'd come find me. One day I was walking near our house and a guy approached me. He asked, "Do you want Yayo [cocaine]?" That was all it took. I started calling him to get my stuff. He was a good pusher and lived super close to my house. He was involved with gangs, not a nice guy in any way.

My addiction was so bad that I asked if I could work for him. I started doing deliveries and got myself into some really hairy situations. I'd ride my bike to his house, get the drugs, take them to the customer, and bring back the money. I was paid in drugs, which was how I supported my habit. I was held up at gunpoint and knifepoint. I was mugged many times. That made me more paranoid: no surprise. I was convinced people were trying to kill me, and all kinds of crazy stuff.

My friends were worried about me. They knew I was into heavier drugs now, and working for drugs, and they didn't like it at all. I'd be calling my dealer and they'd be like, "Hey man, are you sure you want to be doing this? Shouldn't you maybe take a break today?" or "Don't you think about stopping?" I told my friends, "Look, I'm an addict. I think I'm going to be this way forever."

The paranoia just got worse

As I later learned, addiction is a kind of psychological disorder. It's obsessive. You just keep thinking about the drug. You're driven to do it and can't stop yourself. After all the coke was gone, I'd be convinced that I must have spilled some on the floor. I'd search for it, getting more and more paranoid, convinced I was being poisoned, absorbing toxins from the floor of my basement.

The truth is, I wanted to stop. The drugs weren't doing anything to numb my anxiety anymore; they were just making it way worse. I was sick of my lifestyle and I was tired of spending my days scoring drugs. I told my parents many times that I wanted to stop, but I just couldn't.

My dad felt guilty for allowing me to smoke dope in the first place. He may still blame himself. I don't look at it that way. I made my own choices. I pawned my favorite guitar to get drug money. I did manipulative things. I don't think it was my parents' fault in any sense. Anyway, it was my mom's hanging in there with me for those years that gave me a chance at recovery.

I wanted to stop

Reducing the harm

At this point I was nineteen and had been doing cocaine for nearly three years. About six months after I left my last school, my mom found out about a recovery program for adolescents. She coaxed me into going to the orientation program, just to check it out.

I had tried rehab programs before but they never worked for me. They were abstinence-based and I felt very stigmatized and manipulated. But this one had a "harm reduction" philosophy. The cool thing about harm reduction is that it doesn't stigmatize or moralize. But it recognizes the potential harm and aims to reduce it, through a combination of compassion, intervention, education, and peer support. I thought this sounded amazing and signed right up. I took high school classes in the morning. Going to a school where there weren't dealers around made a big difference. That eliminated both the opportunity and the pressure to get high. I deleted my dealer's number.

In the afternoon I went to a support group with six other kids, all of us awkward, dealing with the same things. I loved that I could set my own goals and work toward them at my own pace. We became a really close-knit community. It was inspiring how much we all supported each other.

I won't lie. I relapsed a few times, but no one was breathing down my neck with a urine-test kit in hand. Instead of yelling at me, the counselors said, "Wow! I'm really sorry to hear that. What can we do to prevent this from happening in the future?" I'm a big advocate of harm reduction. I honestly think it (and my mom) saved my life.

Self-destruction was not the answer

During my recovery, I had to deal with my mental health, which was an underlying part of my drug addiction. As I started to get free of cocaine, I started feeling really, really anxious, in a way I never had before. I washed my hands until my skin was raw. I was afraid to go to public places because I thought I'd get injured. I knew I had severe anxiety, but I didn't know until then that I also had a specific form of it, obsessive-compulsive disorder, or OCD. I kept washing my hands because it was a compulsion. It was also why I was so vulnerable to addiction in the first place.

I nurtured my interests

To treat my OCD and other anxieties, I started cognitive behavioral therapy, a type of therapy that focuses on how our thoughts cause our feelings and our actions. It helped me learn to think differently and to find ways of coping that didn't rely on substances. I nurtured my interests in guitar playing and skateboarding, and used them to take my mind off my emotional distress.

The skateboarding really helped me. The incentive of learning a cool trick gave me a reason to leave the house. I was afraid of going around construction sites or anyplace I'd get dirty or breathe in dust, so we made a schedule where I'd skateboard for five minutes on Monday outside a place that I was frightened of. Then ten minutes on Tuesday, and twenty minutes on Wednesday, gradually increasing the amount of time until I got comfortable there. As I did that, I picked up momentum. I got stronger and more confident to the point where now I don't notice my OCD much. I still obsess about some things, but I no longer have a problem living a full life—and I've been off cocaine for five years.

Destroying yourself is not the best way to fight your problems. I've lost a lot of friends to drugs and alcohol. I took serious risks doing what I did.

No one reason can explain why a person becomes an addict. And there's no single factor involved in their recovery. Along with the support of my mom and a recovery program that didn't judge me, I got treatment for my anxiety. These factors, combined with the will to live, were my lifesavers.

If you're not happy with some aspect of your behavior, it's important to know that you can change it. Have a goal, find a supportive community, and just don't give up.

The Bathroom Chronicles

=—◉—=

STACEY

Our pug Spencer had a thing about thunder. Before we could even tell a storm was coming, he'd cower and whimper, and if we weren't around to pat him, he'd poop in the basement. I knew how Spencer felt. Except it wasn't thunder that scared me. It was people finding fault with me. If I saw that coming, I'd end up hugging the toilet.

It took me a while to realize that not everyone had this same reaction. In ninth grade my friend Jenna was horsing around in Gym, not paying attention. The teacher was a no-nonsense drill sergeant and she'd had enough.

"You're really a waste of time, aren't you?" she said, teed off.

Jenna's face turned blotchy red, but she didn't say anything and started following the drills. At lunch, I asked Jenna if she was okay.

"Okay about what?" she said.

"Aren't you mortified?"

"Why should I be?"

At first I thought she was kidding, but she wasn't. She'd been embarrassed at the moment but she was over it now.

Wow. If it had been me, that moment would have been on endless replay. I would have thought, *That teacher will tell my parents. They'll get mad at me and start to argue, and then they'll end up divorced and it'll be all my fault.* In real life, my mom and dad were actually pretty laid-back. I piled on the pressure all by myself.

Pressure cooker

Back in middle school, I was a skinny kid with big bags under my eyes. Even though I ate plenty, I looked like a scarecrow. That meant I got teased—a lot. It didn't matter that I was a top student; I always felt different. Even walking in the halls made me anxious. I couldn't shake the negative thoughts. *People are staring at me. I don't belong here.* My iPod earbuds were a great foil; I'd stick them in between classes to fend off casual encounters. I applied to a specialized arts high school just to avoid the catty girls who liked to pick on me.

My new school was a big, bustling place with amazing arts facilities and a fully equipped theater. There were fewer cliques to worry about and I made some good friends. But academically it was a whole different world. To get an A you had to go above and beyond. I wasn't happy with 80s. I wanted 90s. Anything less made me feel like a failure.

My parents didn't get why I was so driven. They would say, "Don't worry about it. Whatever mark you get, we'll still love you!" I didn't listen. Instead I'd freak out. Maybe I wasn't the most popular kid but I *was* one of the smarter people. I just had to hold on to that.

I was your classic stressed-out teenager. My constant worry about my grade point average gave me headaches and made me snap at my friends. Fighting with Mom and Dad made me break out in rashes or feel sick to my stomach. They chalked it up to my being "high-strung."

The way I did my schoolwork made things worse. My preoccupation with grades made me put off doing homework. I'd wait till the last minute to start a project and then push, push, push late into the night. Most of the time I pulled it off, so I'd convinced myself that I worked best under pressure. But sometimes I'd have a meltdown around midnight and end up in the bathroom throwing up.

In the second half of freshman year, I had strange bouts of sharp stomach pain, what seemed like food poisoning. One morning, before a math test, I threw up so much that I ended up in the emergency room. The doctors said it was something I ate, dosed me with medicine, and sent me home. When it happened again sophomore year, no one connected the dots. Certainly not me: I already had enough to worry about.

Disaster strikes

By junior year the stakes had gotten higher. That spring I had a heavy workload in Biology and Chemistry, which I loved, and in French, which I didn't. Exams were coming, and I was gearing up for my usual all-nighters. On top of that I was the stage manager of the school's huge drama production. The drama teacher was good but tough. I had heard that she screamed at stage managers who didn't work quickly enough during rehearsals. This time I didn't dare procrastinate. I came to the first major rehearsal prepared—and really nervous.

Part of my job was directing the stagehands. When they all showed up late, I could taste bile in my throat. "Get your asses in gear!" I shrieked. They reacted by spending the rest of the afternoon in slow motion. That rehearsal was a disaster. I ended up moving most of the sets myself. The teacher screamed at me. By the end of the day I was in tears.

When I got home that night, I was a wreck. My ego was shot and I felt like somebody was turning a corkscrew in my gut. I took Spencer to bed with me to calm me down, but by midnight the pain was so bad that my parents rushed me to the ER. After twenty-four hours the doctors had a name for what was wrong. I had Crohn's disease, a chronic inflammation of the bowel that alternates between flare-ups and periods of calm. No one knows the cause and you can't cure it. One thing I know for sure: it's aggravated by stress.

Being able to put a name to what was going on was a huge help. It gave me something real to focus on. A lot of people want to hide the fact that they have Crohn's because it's a "poop" disease. In spite of being easily mortified by most things, I didn't mind telling my close friends all the details, and they were nice about it. Even the drama teacher was supportive.

I got through the school year without any more flare-ups, but by summer it was obvious that my body had hit some kind of breaking point. Before, my stomach episodes had happened about twice a year. Now they were coming more often. That ratcheted up my stress, big-time.

Enough already

I was worried about the big year ahead—senior year. I would have a heavy course load and I needed good grades to get into a top college. The first week of school I saw my doctors for what I thought was a routine checkup. It turned out to be anything but. I had abscesses—infected swellings—in my gut. I had to stay in the hospital for two weeks. I was furious. I felt fine! Didn't they get that I was missing the beginning of school?

Back home, things weren't much better. Every night I was hooked up to a pump for twelve hours, which delivered oceans of a special formula to heal the abscesses. For six weeks I wasn't allowed to eat *anything*; I could only drink clear fluids.

The steroids in my meds gave me a moon face. I went from a size 24 to a size 30 pants overnight. Classmates would ask, "Why do you look that way? Did you get your wisdom teeth out? Why do you keep missing school?"

As I struggled with my overdue homework, I couldn't shake the feeling of already being way behind. *You'll never catch up, you'll never catch up* kept buzzing in my head. I was afraid I might not graduate. I'd assumed the medications would do the trick, but my stomach problems only escalated.

Missing out

One night I was lying in bed wondering how my senior year could get any worse when Jenna called. She went on and on about her boy problems until I blurted out, "You don't have a clue what a real problem is!"

Jenna's voice changed and she said she'd call me later. I punched the Off button and cried. Spencer came in and licked my hand.

Jenna forgave me, and my other friends were nice enough, but I was lonely. I felt like I'd left them behind on another planet while I was on the *Spaceship Crohn's*. Sleepovers? Parties? Forget about it. I had to hook up at 7:30 p.m. and couldn't unhook until 7:30 a.m. I was missing out on everything.

That month I had my worst Thanksgiving ever. It was pretty depressing watching everyone eat mounds of incredible-smelling food. Then my mom brought out a surprise dish just for me— Jell-O in the shape of a turkey. I felt a lump in my throat. I forced myself to laugh so I wouldn't cry.

Disaster strikes again

The nightly hookups were a huge drag, and they didn't even seem to help. Four weeks in, I woke up in the middle of the night with the worst pain I'd ever felt, like my intestines were twisted inside out. It was so bad I couldn't get out of bed. I called out to my parents. I clanged the bell they had put beside my bed for emergencies. I threw the books on my night table at the door. Nothing. After what seemed like forever, my mom went to the bathroom, heard me yelling, and rushed in.

If I had known what was actually happening, I would have been even more panicked. My large intestine was leaking into my insides. That's an emergency, life-threatening if not treated within twenty-four hours. I went straight into surgery so they could take out the diseased part of my bowel.

The crisis was over. I could eat again, and I could stop taking the steroids that had made me look like a puffy alien. The bad news was that for three months I would have to wear an "ostomy" (poop) bag to school, while my bowel healed. Even though it was temporary, it was pretty embarrassing, one more blow to my fragile seventeen-year-old self. I was certainly not about to go on any dates.

My "aha" moment

I got an unlikely moment of relief from what began as a total disaster. One day my ostomy bag burst in class. Before anyone got wind of the mess, I rushed to the handicapped bathroom and locked the door. Then, just as I peeled off my jeans, the fire alarm went off. I panicked. Then I caught sight of myself in the mirror and I realized how ridiculous it all was. A switch went on in my head and I had to smile. I took my chances that the school wasn't burning down and stayed put. I called my mom from the bathroom and sneaked out a back exit, where she was waiting for me. We had a good laugh on the way home. I figured since it was one of those stories that was *going* to be funny, I might as well laugh now.

We had a good laugh

That incident helped me come to terms with reality: the fact was, I had an incurable disease, Crohn's. And there was a connection between my Crohn's and my stress. I *had* to figure out how to lessen my anxiety. My life depended on it.

Mind shift

Like it or not, I had to grow up fast. While my body healed, another big change was taking place: slowly I began to make a new life. I drifted away from the friends I'd had before, except for one who had bad scoliosis. She and I became closer than ever. And I became good friends with a boy and girl with Crohn's I'd met in the hospital. We hung out and even went to some medical fund-raisers together.

I could no longer kid myself that leaving things to the last minute was a good idea. I made time for things that calmed me down, like walking Spencer. I made sure I spent at least a half hour with him every day. And then there was humor. I'd always had a good instinct for the absurd, but now I knew how vital it was to step back and find something to laugh at. Turning an awful situation into a funny story made the experience bearable, and kept me from becoming withdrawn or stressed out.

The driven side of my personality, my brittleness and impatience, began to fade. About halfway through senior year one of my friends commented, "You're a lot nicer to be around. You're more relaxed now." It had happened so gradually I hadn't even noticed.

I still had my moments: when I realized I had tons of community service hours (required of all high school students) to complete by the end of the year, I freaked out. *Oh my God, after all I've been through, I'm not going to graduate!* The old me would have found a volunteer job and crammed in the dozens of hours even if I made myself sick. Instead, I thought, *This is silly. I'll just go to the guidance counselor and see what we can figure out.* Together we found a solution that didn't involve me taking on too much. I recognized that I couldn't do it all.

I realized how much I'd changed when prom time came. For most of senior year, I hadn't spent much time hanging out with my old friends, though we still meant a lot to each other. On prom night there were only so many spots in their limo. I was the odd one out. The old me would have been crushed. Instead, I found another group of friends to go with, and we had a great time.

Being sick put things in perspective. It helped me learn how to get a grip on my anxiety. And the coping strategies I developed for my anxiety helped me get well.

Oh, this *is what I was meant to do*

My weeks in the hospital made me dig even more into biology and chemistry, which I already loved. I talked about it a lot with the people in the hospital, and they said I should be a nurse. I couldn't see that. "No, no," I said, "I want to go into business and marketing." Three years into a college business program I finally saw the light.

I was in remission at the time and I wanted to stay that way. I was on a special diet and consumed with all things health-related. It dawned on me that being a nurse would be the best way to help myself stay well, and to do the same for others. This would never have occurred to me if I hadn't become ill. Right away I applied to nursing school. I've been at it for two years, and I've never looked back. This is what I'm meant to do. I'm completely passionate about it.

I wouldn't wish Crohn's disease on anyone. But in a way I feel lucky. My hospital emergency finally got me to deal with my anxiety problems, and I'm a way more relaxed person now. I still like being an A student but I don't take on nearly as much as I did back then. Grad school friends ask, "Why aren't you stressed out about this like we are?" I say, "I can't be. It will put me in the hospital. It's just that simple."

War Story

HAMID

My family has lived through years of war, fear, and loss. Anxiety is always with us.

It started in Kashmir, a place so beautiful it's called heaven on earth. But there's no such thing as heavenly peace there. For as long as my grandparents have been alive, India, Pakistan, and China have been vying for control of the country.

In the Neelum Valley, where my parents married and had a young family, violence was on the rise. Weapons and militants were pouring over the border from Afghanistan, which had just ended a nine-year war with the Soviet Union. There were street protests, bombings, kidnappings, and shootings.

The growing insurgency frightened my parents. Worried about the family's future in Kashmir, they fled with my two sisters to Peshawar, a city in northern Pakistan, where my mother had relatives. My parents were rebuilding their lives when my older brother, Akbar, and I were born, followed by two more daughters.

My unstable future

I was ten years old when another catastrophe landed on our heads. After Osama bin Laden brought down the twin towers in New York, the US and UK attacked Afghanistan, just over the border from Peshawar. In the blink of an eye, our region became a battle zone. Our house wasn't a target of the bombs, but we were very close to some targets. The Taliban, a militant religious group that was fighting for control of territory in Pakistan and Afghanistan, had missiles and the Americans bombarded them. The closeness of the bombs terrified me, and made me faint. Our doors would shake so much all the locks would break. It was a crisis for our entire family.

> It was a crisis for our entire family

My father wasn't involved in politics or fighting. One of my mother's relatives was an extremist, though, with ties to the Taliban. We didn't know anything about what "Uncle" did but my parents didn't want us involved, whatever it was.

The spillover from the war in Afghanistan would die down for a while, then pick up again. In spite of the turmoil, life went on. Akbar and I were close, traveling to school, taking English classes, and playing cricket together. As the two sons, we had special roles in the family: helping our father with his work and doing errands in the market and downtown. We agreed: we didn't want to be fighters.

One day, Uncle came to see us. My father and Akbar received him and I served tea and desserts. Uncle said to Akbar, "I want you and Hamid to join us in fighting, and choose the right way. This is how you boys should start your life." My father put him off, telling him, "We want the boys to finish high school. Then we'll decide. They're not old enough." It didn't matter: in Uncle's eyes, we were old enough.

A week later Uncle came to talk to us again. This time my

father got mad. He said, "These are my sons. Respect our wishes. Leave us alone!" Uncle left very angry. He told Akbar, "We won't let you boys go. You'll see." We knew he meant it. We were all scared but not sure what to do.

A few weeks later, Akbar went down to the market. He never came back.

For two months we searched the city and the surrounding villages with our friends and neighbors. When we contacted the authorities, they all said, "Why should I get killed for helping you?" They were scared of the Taliban, too. We appealed to Uncle but he claimed he had no information. We hoped that Akbar had only been kidnapped and we'd get a ransom call. But no call came.

Our lives seemed normal. My father went to work and I went to school but nothing was the same. We were always cautious, always afraid. Akbar's absence left a hole in my heart. I missed him most in the evenings when we used to eat and do homework together. I had to believe he'd come home, but my parents knew the truth: Akbar didn't have a chance. We never heard from him again.

Friends told us, "You should leave Pakistan. It's not safe for you here." After a lot of talking, my parents decided that we needed to go to the West, and since I was in the most danger, I would leave first. "You're the only son we have left," my father said. "We don't want anything to happen to you." I didn't want to leave but my father insisted. The idea of being separated from my family, even for a few weeks, filled me with dread. But I had no inkling of what was to come.

Desperate times

We didn't have passports, and going to the authorities for official documents was too dangerous. Unofficially, my parents found an agent who charged thousands of dollars to forge documents and get me a plane ticket to Canada. My parents and sisters would leave as soon as they could raise the money for more documents.

The agent gave me two fake passports. One British, to get me out of Pakistan and through my first stop, and one Pakistani, which the agent said I'd need in the West. I arrived at my first stop, in Ukraine, with my Pakistani passport in one pocket and the fake British passport in the other. The immigration officer ordered me to empty my pockets. "Hands up," he said. I had my Pakistani passport in one hand and the British one in my other hand. I was sweating and my heart was throbbing. It was impossible to hide how scared I was.

> I was sweating and my heart was throbbing

He patted me down and saw I had no weapons. Instead of saying, "What is in your hands? Why do you have two passports?" he said, "You can go." I think it was God or my prayers that saved me.

The Pakistani forger had told me to throw the British passport in the toilet once I got to the West. "When you get to Canada," he said, "tell them you are from Pakistan." I didn't follow his advice. I threw the Pakistani passport away instead. When the plane landed on the tarmac, I was surprised that we were all told to stay in our seats. Then two big immigration officers came directly to my seat and asked for my passport. I gave them the British passport and they said, "Come with us." Everyone on the plane was looking at me. I was scared. I was embarrassed. I didn't know what would happen next.

"Where are you from?" one of the men asked me.

"I'm British," I said in my best English.

"What's your name?"

I faltered because I didn't know what to say. My British passport had a different name.

The officer grabbed me and pushed me. "Come on, man,"

he said. "You're wasting our time and yours. You know you're a refugee. Just tell us the truth."

"Then why are you pushing me?" I demanded. I was paralyzed by anger and fear. My mouth was so dry I couldn't have talked if I'd wanted to.

Terrified and homesick

"Water," I said. "Please, water, and I'll tell you everything." They asked my name again. This time I told them the truth, and admitted that I was from Pakistan. By now it was midnight. The officer gave me water and I slept, sure I would be put on a plane and deported the next morning.

That was the least of my worries. I was sad and preoccupied with home. In my culture, if you are the oldest son, you look after the whole family. When my dad was away, Akbar was responsible. Now I was the oldest son—thousands of miles from home, alone, and filled with regret. I hadn't done enough to help them. I had no idea whether they were safe or in danger.

The immigration officials questioned me for sixteen hours. Finally they decided I had left Pakistan for a good reason. But I had no identity because I had thrown away the wrong passport.

I managed to reach a family friend in Peshawar who had been given a copy of my birth certificate for safekeeping, and a few hours later he faxed it to the immigration office. He also told me that my family had left but he didn't know where they'd gone. That made me feel worse. I had no way to contact them. We never used e-mail at home and no one in my family had a cell phone. I was sick with fear that I'd never see them again. I was completely and utterly alone.

I fell asleep on an airport bench, exhausted by weeks of constant stress. An immigration officer shook me awake sometime later.

"Hamid, you're free to go," she said. "Don't worry about anything. We'll help you."

I learned that I could stay in the country for up to five years, or until my request for asylum was processed.

A new life, alone

I never shared my real feelings

I stayed in a shelter for a month while I looked for a place to live. A refugee organization helped me find a doctor and a high school. Even with all the help, I felt stressed and depressed. I had no appetite and lost weight. My thick black hair started falling out. At my new school I felt dizzy and exhausted. It was hard to concentrate. I couldn't relate to people my own age; how could they understand what I had been through? I'd just turned seventeen and had never been on my own before: my parents had organized my time, fed me, cleaned my clothes, everything. I had very little money and felt completely lost, wondering, *What should I do first? What should I do next?* I had trouble remembering appointments and I missed deadlines. Only part of my brain was in Canada. The rest was half a world away.

Over time I made friends. One day at school, a guy came over to me and said, "Brother, are you from Pakistan?" It turned out that we'd grown up a few miles from each other! We started going to mosque together and through him I made more friends, from India, Portugal, all over the place.

On the outside I was adjusting. But I never shared my real feelings, not even with friends. If you were to ask them about me they would say, *He's very tough.* They never saw me sad or crying. But I didn't feel tough. I felt hopeless. I kept imagining my brother's abduction, his terror and pain. Had the same thing happened to my sisters, my parents? The agent's phone had been

disconnected. None of our old neighbors had heard from my family. I had no answers.

Months passed. My emotions flew in every direction. I was suspicious one minute, in a rage the next. I can't even describe the pain. I thought of suicide, but then I'd think of my family. What if I was the only person who could help them?

I went through the motions of high school, studying English, going to martial arts class. But inside I was sick, sick with longing for Akbar, for my family, for my country. I got so desperate I wanted to leave Canada and start searching for them. "Don't go," my friends said. "Try to be patient." In truth, I had no idea where to go.

Nights were the worst. I relived my anxiety in horrible, violent dreams. I saw my father's dead body. Wild dogs chased me. My little sister was covered in blood. I'd wake up in the middle of the night screaming, soaked in sweat, absolutely terrified. That happened hundreds of times.

Finally, news of my family!

More than a year passed without any word. I got through high school and started a premed course. I had decided to become a doctor. I was on a computer in the library one day when I saw an e-mail from a friend in Pakistan who had been searching for information about my family all this time; he had found a phone number. They were in Kashmir!

I ran through the library, searching for a pay phone. My hand shook as I punched in the number. My mother answered and I greeted her. She gasped in shock, and when she called out my name I heard my sister scream in the background. My mother was crying so hard she couldn't speak. When she finally recovered she said, "I've found my world!"

I stood there sobbing like a kid. I talked to my sisters and my father, and my dad told me the story of what had happened to them. As soon as I left, they felt very vulnerable so they went into hiding while my father sold what property he could. The agent thought if they left Pakistan by air it would raise suspicion, so he sent them overland to Turkey. But they were stopped at the border and had to turn around. Rather than risk returning to Peshawar, they went back to Kashmir.

They were alive, but hearing how hard their lives were brought a lot of new worries. I felt guilty that I was the one who had made it to the safety of Canada. At the same time I thought, *If I wasn't here, what would have happened to me? At least here I can work and send money every month.*

I had to see my family or I'd never have any peace. I borrowed money from friends and eventually received permission to leave Canada. In Kashmir I found my parents living in poverty. What little money they had had left after paying the agent and escaping Pakistan was long gone, and because the Taliban was active in Kashmir, they still felt vulnerable.

Once, we'd lived in a comfortable house with a pretty garden and my father had had a good income. Now he spent his days looking for any kind of work. Both my parents had lost a lot of weight. My sisters had nightmares and cried often. They had all changed so much in the years we'd been apart. I saw their hopelessness.

Seeing my family profoundly shocked me. Everything in my old world had changed. It was hard to leave them behind and come back to Canada, where I felt like a stranger all over again. It was September and I had to start school. For three months I couldn't focus at all and I even wrote my exams without studying. I was too stressed to eat. I wouldn't talk to anyone and had a hard time following conversations.

My old world had changed

My only thought was to earn money. I took a leave from school and accepted all the jobs I could find. I bussed tables, washed windows, and cleaned houses. I had the energy to work two or three times harder than the average person because I was sure my family's survival depended on it.

Accepting my anxiety

Anxiety is part of me now; it never goes away. Each time I talk to my parents, it seems there is something new to worry about. My father sees someone he knows at the grocery store; he becomes afraid and wants to move the family again. News like that used to send me into a panic but it doesn't paralyze me anymore. I've learned to tolerate it. I have no choice.

I'm back in my premed program, earning money at part-time jobs. I live off a small government stipend and send my parents every dollar I earn. My refugee application was finally approved:

I can stay in Canada for as long as I choose. My deepest wish is to sponsor my family to join me here. To do that I need a well-paying job.

Sometimes I volunteer as a speaker at the refugee center that I have relied on for advice and counseling since I got here four years ago. I talk about families separated and made poor by war. I talk about the trauma of leaving home and being alone in another country. Sharing my story gives me hope. I've learned that the more people understand, the more caring they are. I don't feel so alone.

I'm twenty years old, and some days, my dark memories and worries make me feel like I'm one hundred. But I'm determined to become a doctor and help my family. I'll get there, one day at a time.

Afterword

Mind racing ... heart pounding ... panicked. *Why is this happening? I'm walking into a classroom, not a lion's cage, but that's what it feels like.*

Anxiety can be paralyzing. It can come on suddenly and "attack," or be a constant current of discomfort. Its causes can be obvious or subtle. It can lead you to avoid situations that others don't, to develop irrational fears, to become trapped by a need to perform illogical rituals. It can affect you mildly and just be an annoyance, or severely and make you feel helpless.

You may feel alone, but you're not. Millions of people suffer from anxiety.

Why you? Genetics may have predisposed you to be overly anxious, or maybe life experiences conditioned you to react this way. Regardless, there are many approaches to help decrease your suffering. The goal is to gain the ability to live your life without anxiety getting in the way.

The first line of defense is physical. When you're anxious, your body becomes tense. When you stay tense, it reinforces to your brain that there is a threat present—a reason to stay tense and alert. By practicing relaxation techniques like deep breathing and muscle relaxation, you can dial down your anxiety level and decompress enough to focus on your thoughts.

Anxiety is a feeling, and behind every feeling are thoughts. Sometimes we know exactly what we're thinking at the time a feeling comes over us; other times it takes some detective work. If you have significant anxiety, you may have developed negative patterns in the way you think. You may assume the worst about situations or how people judge you, catastrophize potential outcomes, or assign yourself a self-defeating label (e.g., "I'm stupid") rather than looking at your individual behaviors ("I made a mistake").

Part of establishing more realistic thinking includes developing a healthy perspective. Fight the urge to follow the herd. Instead, focus on what's best for you. Learn to let go of comparing yourself to others, focus on your efforts rather than the outcome, and give yourself permission to follow a different path if it feels more like you.

If you are ready to seek help from a professional, look for a psychologist or therapist trained in cognitive behavioral therapy (CBT), one of the best-targeted treatments for anxiety. Your therapist will help you develop an awareness of the way you approach situations and how you think about them. She or he will teach you to change the patterns that are working against you, and to successfully approach (rather than avoid) anxiety-provoking situations. She or he can also help you resolve any emotional or relationship issues that may be contributing to your anxiety.

If you are too anxious to tune into your thoughts or are suffering greatly, you may be referred to a psychiatrist, who will let you know if medication may be helpful. Some medications keep your anxiety level down every day; others are taken only when needed. Medication helps get you to a point where other approaches can work, and the combination of medication and CBT can be a very effective treatment for anxiety. If you are prescribed medication, you must continue to see your psychiatrist for monitoring. Communicate any effects you notice, whether positive or negative. Work together with your psychiatrist, so he or she can determine the safest and most effective medication regimen for you.

Maintaining a healthy lifestyle, including exercise, nutrition, sleep, and minimizing caffeine (which raises anxiety in some people), can lower your anxiety. It's also helpful to create space between you and your stressors. Take time for calmness—some like meditation, imagery exercises, or yoga; others get lost in books or music. Establishing interests and hobbies is healthy, too.

Finally, seek support. Family, peers, mentors, and support groups can be invaluable.

What helps you? Be open to finding out. Understand that you can move from feeling helpless to being empowered and in control of the anxiety that has been controlling you.

> Stacie B. Isenberg, Psy.D.
> Clinical Psychologist, Private Practice
> Director, Child & Adolescent Services,
> The Ross Center for Anxiety and
> Related Disorders, Washington, D.C.

Resources

Learning about anxiety and how to manage it is rather like a quest. You may find these books and websites to be useful guides along your journey. A growing number of novels feature characters who are dealing with anxiety in some form. Workbooks offer step-by-step instruction in methods of controlling anxiety, such as cognitive behavioral therapy (CBT) and meditation. Some websites are geared specifically to teenagers; others focus on specific types of anxiety.

BOOKS

FICTION

Buffie, Margaret. *Angels Turn Their Backs*. Toronto: Kids Can Press, 1998.

Chbosky, Stephen. *The Perks of Being a Wallflower*. New York: Gallery Books, 1999.

Colasanti, Susane. *Waiting for You*. New York: Viking/Penguin, 2009.

Hesser, Terry Spencer. *Kissing Doorknobs*. New York: Laurel Leaf Books, 1998.

McGowan, Anthony. *The Knife That Killed Me*. New York: Random House, 2008.

Sanchez, Alex. *Bait*. New York: Simon & Schuster, 2009.

Tashjian, Janet. *Multiple Choice*. New York: Henry Holt, 1999.

Walters, Eric. *Wounded*. Toronto: Penguin, 2009.

Zusak, Mark. *The Book Thief*. New York: Knopf, 2005.

NON-FICTION

Acres, David. *Passing Exams Without Anxiety*. Philadelphia: Trans-Atlantic Publications, 1998.

Adderholdt, Miriam and Jan Goldberg. *Perfectionism: What's Bad About Being Too Good?* Minneapolis: Free Spirit Publishing, 1999.

Antony, Martin and Richard Swinson. *The Shyness and Social Anxiety Workbook: Proven, Step-by-Step Techniques for Overcoming Your Fear, 2nd Edition*. Oakland: New Harbinger, 2008.

Antony, Martin and Richard Swinson. *When Perfect Isn't Good Enough: Strategies for Coping with Perfectionism, 2nd Edition*. Oakland: New Harbinger, 2009.

Bourne, Edmund J. *The Anxiety and Phobia Workbook, 4th Edition*. Oakland: New Harbinger, 2010.

Ford, Emily, Michael Liebowitz, and Linda W. Andrews. *What You Must Think of Me: A Firsthand Account of One Teenager's Experience with Social Anxiety Disorder*. New York: Oxford University Press, 2007.

Greenberger, Dennis and Christine A. Padesky Ph.D. *Mind Over Mood: Change How You Feel by Changing the Way You Think*. New York: Guilford Press, 1995.

Hope, Debra, Richard Heimberg, and Cynthia Turk. *Managing Social Anxiety: A Cognitive-Behavioral Therapy Approach, 2nd Edition*. Oxford: Oxford University Press, 2010.

Kant, J.D., Martin E. Franklin, and Linda Wasmer Andrews. *The Thought That Counts: A Firsthand Account of One Teenager's Experience with Obsessive-Compulsive Disorder*. New York: Oxford University Press, 2008.

Kendall, Philip C., Muniya Choudhury, Jennifer Hudson, and Alicia Webb. *"The C.A.T. Project" Workbook for the Cognitive-Behavioral Treatment of Anxious Adolescents*. Ardmore, PA: Workbook Publishing, 2002.

Leahy, Robert. *The Worry Cure: Seven Steps to Stop Worry from Stopping You*. New York: Three Rivers Press, a Division of Random House, 2005.

Lee, Jordan and Carolyn Simpson. *Coping with Anxiety and Panic Attacks*. New York: Rosen Publishing Group, 1997.

Maloney, Michael and Rachel Kranz. *Straight Talk About Anxiety and Depression*. New York: Facts on File, 1993.

March, John and Karen Mulle. *OCD in Children and Adolescents: A Cognitive-Behavioral Treatment Manual*. New York: Guilford Press, 1998.

Schab, Lisa. *The Anxiety Workbook for Teens: Activities to Help You Deal with Anxiety and Worry*. Oakland: New Harbinger Publications, 2008.

Smith, Daniel. *Monkey Mind: A Memoir of Anxiety*. New York: Simon and Schuster, 2012.

Wilson, R. Reid. *Facing Panic: Self-Help for People with Panic Attacks*. Silver Spring, MD: ADAA, 2003.

FOR YOUR PARENTS

Chansky, T.E. *Freeing Your Child From Anxiety*. New York: Broadway Books, 2004.

Chansky, T.E. *Freeing Your Child From Negative Thinking*. Cambridge, MA: Da Capo Lifelong Books, 2008.

Chansky, T.E. *Freeing Your Child From Obsessive-Compulsive Disorder*. New York: Crown Publishing Group, 2001.

Foa, Edna B. and Linda Wasmer Andrews. *If Your Adolescent Has an Anxiety Disorder: An Essential Resource for Parents*. New York: Oxford University Press, 2006.

Manassis, Katharina. *Keys to Parenting Your Anxious Child*. New York: Barron's Educational Series, 1996.

Rapee, Ronald M., Ann Wignall, Susan H. Spence, Vanessa Cobham, and Heidi Lyneham, Ph.D. *Helping Your Anxious Child: A Step-by-Step Guide for Parents*. Oakland: New Harbinger, 2008.

Spencer, Elizabeth D., Robert DuPont, and Caroline DuPont. *The Anxiety Cure for Kids: A Guide for Parents.* Hoboken, NJ: John Wiley & Sons, 2003.

AUDIO

Karapetian Alvord, Mary, Bonnie Zucker, and Bryce Alvord. *Relaxation and Self-Regulation Techniques for Children and Teens: Mastering the Mind-Body Connection* (Audio CD). Champaign, IL: Research Press, 2011.

WEBSITES AND HOTLINES

FOR TEENS

Cope Care Deal: A mental health site for teens. www.copecaredeal.org

Kids Help Phone: Canada's free, round-the-clock phone counseling service (1-800-668-6868) for kids twenty and under, with information on anxiety, bullying, depression, and abuse. www.kidshelpphone.ca

Mind Your Mind: An award-winning online youth and professional community aimed at reducing the stigma of mental illness. www.mindyourmind.ca

National Mental Health Association Hotline: A network of crisis centers in 50 states. Free and confidential emotional support to people in suicidal crisis, and anyone suffering from emotional distress. 24 hours a day, seven days a week, 800-273-TALK (8255).The website provides links to mental health resources state-by-state. www.nmha.org

Youth America Hotline: Toll-free, peer-to-peer hotline network, 1-877-YOUTHLINE (968-8454), linking callers to community based peer counseling hotlines across the U.S. The website offers specific information about a variety of issues including stress/anxiety, depression, and suicide. www.youthline.us

GENERAL

American Academy of Child and Adolescent Psychiatry:
www.aacap.org

The American Psychological Association: www.APA.org

Magination Press (APA's publisher): www.maginationpress.com

Anxiety and Depression Association of America: www.adaa.org

Anxiety Disorders Association of Canada: www.anxietycanada.ca

Association for Behavioral and Cognitive Therapies:
www.abct.org

The National Association of School Psychologists:
www.nasponline.org

The National Institute of Mental Health: www.nimh.nih.gov

Psych Central: www.psychcentral.com

WorryWiseKids: www.worrywisekids.org

SOCIAL ANXIETY

Madison Institute of Medicine:
www.socialanxiety.factsforhealth.org

OBSESSIVE COMPULSIVE DISORDER

International OCD Foundation: www.ocfoundation.org

The National Institute of Mental Health:
www.nimh.nih.gov/health/topics/obsessive-compulsive-disorder-ocd/index.shtml

PTSD

Madison Institute of Medicine: www.ptsd.factsforhealth.org

PTSD Alliance Resource Center: ptsdalliance.org

The National Child Traumatic Stress Network: www.nctsnet.org